SKILL
SHARPENERS

Third Edition

JUDY DeFILIPPO
CHARLES SKIDMORE

Longman

Judy DeFilippo supervises MATESL student teachers at Simmons College in Boston, Massachusetts. She is the author of *Lifeskills 1, 2,* and *3* and co-author of *Grammar Plus.*

Charles Skidmore is the principal of Arlington High School in Arlington, Massachusetts. He has taught and supervised the teaching of English as a Second Language for the past twenty-five years. He also serves as adjunct faculty in the Lynch School of Education at Boston College.

Pearson Education, 10 Bank Street, White Plains, NY 10606

Vice president, primary and secondary editorial: Ed Lamprich
Senior development editor: Virginia Bernard
Vice president, design and production: Rhea Banker
Director of editorial production: Linda Moser
Production supervisor: Melissa Leyva
Associate production editor: Laura Lazzaretti
Marketing managers: Alex Smith/Tania Saiz-Sousa
Senior manufacturing buyer: Dave Dickey
Cover design: Ann France
Cover photo: © Emma Lee/Life File/Getty Images
Text design adaptation: Tracey Munz Cataldo
Text composition: Laserwords
Text font: 11/18 Myriad Roman
Illustrations: Elizabeth Hazelton, Kathleen Todd, Andrew Lange
Photo credits: National Aeronautics and Space Administration,
    p. 2; National Park Service/U.S. Department of the Interior,
    p. 38; Cartoon © David Brown, permission granted by CSL
    NewsCartoon Service, p. 83; Photo by Allan Tannenbaum,
    courtesy The Image Works, Inc., p. 100

ISBN: 0-13-192995-X
Printed in the United States of America
2 3 4 5 6 7 8 9 10–VHG–08 07 06 05

Introduction

The *Skill Sharpeners* series has been especially designed for students whose skills in standard English, especially those skills concerned with literacy, require strengthening. It is directed both toward students whose first language is not English and toward those who need additional practice in standard English grammar and vocabulary. By introducing basic skills tied to classroom subjects in a simple, easy-to-understand grammatical framework, the series helps to prepare these students for success in regular ("mainstream") academic subjects. By developing and reinforcing school and life survival skills, it helps build student confidence and self esteem.

Skills Sharpeners focuses on grammar practice and higher order thinking skills. It provides many content-area readings, biographies, opportunities for students to write, and practice in using formats similar to those of many standardized tests. The third edition updates the content of many pages. The central purpose of the series remains the same, however. *Skill Sharpeners* remains dedicated to helping your students sharpen their skills in all facets of English communication.

With English Language Learners, *Skill Sharpeners* supplements and complements any basic ESL text or series. With these students and with others, *Skill Sharpeners* can also be used to reteach and reinforce specific skills with which students are having or have had difficulty. In addition, it can be used to review and practice grammatical structures and to reinforce, expand, and enrich students' vocabularies.

The grammatical structures and the language objectives in *Skill Sharpeners* follow a systematic, small-step progression with many opportunities for practice, review, and reinforcement. Vocabulary and skill instruction is presented in the context of situations and concepts that have an immediate impact on students' daily lives. Themes and subject matter are directly related to curriculum areas. Reading and study skills are stressed in many pages, and writing skills are carefully developed, starting with single words and sentences and building gradually to paragraphs and stories in a structured, controlled composition sequence.

Skill Sharpeners is an ideal supplement for literature-based or sheltered English classrooms. *Skill Sharpeners* allows for direct teaching of grammar and language skills that most textbooks and novels do not supply. Students do not always intuitively grasp grammar and language rules. *Skill Sharpeners* has been designed to allow students a vehicle for continued practice in these areas.

Using the *Skill Sharpeners*

Because each page or pair of pages of the *Skill Sharpeners* is independent and self contained, the series lends itself to great flexibility of use. Teachers may pick and choose pages that fit the needs of particular students, or they may use the pages in sequential order. Most pages are self-explanatory, and all are easy to use, either in class or as homework assignments. Annotations at the bottom of each page identify the skill or skills being developed and suggest ways to prepare for, introduce, and present the exercise(s) on the page. In most cases, oral practice of the material is suggested before the student is asked to complete the page in writing. Teacher demonstration and student involvement and participation help build a foundation for completing the page successfully and learning the skill.

Skill Sharpeners is divided into thematic units. The first unit of each book is introductory. In *Skill Sharpeners 1*, this unit provides exercises to help students say and write their names and addresses and to familiarize them with basic classroom language, school deportment, the names of school areas and school personnel, and number names. In later books of the series, the first unit serves both to review some of the material taught in earlier books and to provide orientation to the series for students coming to it for the first time.

At the end of each of the *Skill Sharpeners* books is a review of vocabulary and an end-of-book test of grammatical and reading skills. The test, largely in multiple-choice format, not only assesses learning of the skills but also provides additional practice for other multiple-choice tests.

The Table of Contents in each book identifies the skills developed on each page. An Index at the end of the book provides an alphabetical list of language objectives. The language objectives are also displayed prominently at the top of each page.

Skill Sharpeners invites expansion! We encourage you to use them as a springboard and to add activities and exercises that build on those in the books to fill the needs of your own particular students. Used this way, the *Skill Sharpeners* can significantly help to build the confidence and skills that students need to be successful members of the community and successful achievers in subject-area classrooms.

Contents

UNIT 7   Decisions, Decisions

UNIT 8   Be a Good Sport

UNIT 9   On the Job

Language Objective
Ask informational questions using a variety of grammatical structures.

Interview as many classmates as you can to get *Yes* answers to the questions below. Try to get at least one *Yes* answer to each question. Write the name of the student who answers *Yes* to a question on the line after the question, along with any other information needed. Be ready to share your answers with the class.

1. Will you have a birthday soon? When? _____

2. Can you name five U.S. presidents? Who? _____

    _____

3. Would you like to be an astronaut someday? _____

4. Can you name the capital of El Salvador? What is it? _____

5. Do you have three sisters and a brother? _____

6. Are you the oldest in your family? _____

7. Would you like to be a surgeon? _____

8. Can you play a musical instrument? What? _____

9. Can you play tennis or handball? _____

10. Have you ever kissed a dog or a cat? _____

11. Do you have a part time job? What is it? _____

12. Have you ridden in a taxi recently? Where did you go? _____

13. Do you like to watch baseball on TV? _____

14. Have you ever swallowed a fly? _____

15. Have you ever acted in a play? _____

16. Did you ever ride on a rollercoaster? _____

17. Have you ever walked in your sleep? _____

18. Have you ever given a speech to a group? _____

SKILL OBJECTIVES: Interviewing; making an oral report. Ask the class if anyone had a birthday within the past week (month, three months). When was it? Draw a line on the board and write the person's name and the date. Ask other questions (motor boat ride, trip to another city, etc.) and record names and details. Tell students they are going to ask similar questions (those on the page) to classmates; they are to try to get at least one *Yes* answer to each question. Students are to record their answers, then report to the class.

1

Complete the Sentence

Language Objective
Complete sentences with grammatically correct structures.

A Complete each sentence by filling the blank with one word or more than one word that makes sense. Make sure your sentences are correct grammatically.

Example: People here *are / seem / act / aren't* friendly.

(Any of the answers filled in above would be correct. You may be able to think of others, too.)

1. Every day the children _____.

2. Miguel drives carefully, but his brother _____.

3. Right now she _____ in the kitchen.

4. The teacher always _____.

5. He _____ a week ago.

6. She is _____ than he is.

7. In 2004, we _____.

8. Next year we _____.

9. This is the most _____ of them all.

10. Since 2001 he _____.

11. I had an accident while I _____.

12. She has never _____.

13. Carlos wasn't at the game, but his brothers _____.

14. She said _____.

B Fill in each blank space with one word. Be sure your words make sense and are correct grammatically. The first one is done for you.

In July, 1969, astronauts Neil Armstrong and Edwin Aldrin landed _____*on*_____ the moon. They walked, collected rocks, _____ put an American flag there. Two _____ later, in July, 1971, astronauts David Scott and Charles Irwin _____ to the moon and brought with them _____ special "car," the Moon Rover. They _____ the car for five miles. The top speed _____ seven miles per hour.

"Man, oh man!" cried Scott. "What a Grand Prix this is."

SKILL OBJECTIVES: Reviewing grammar; completing a cloze exercise. At the beginning of the course, it is important to find out what grammatical structures your English students have not previously learned. This exercise gives you a fast, useful overview. *Part A:* Tell students to write one or more words that will complete each sentence. Do the example on the board together and ask for other words that might complete it (*appear to be, look, are never,* etc.). Give students as much time as they need. *Part B:* After explaining directions carefully on the board, you may assign this as written work for individuals or pairs. When students have completed it, discuss all possible responses, explaining why some are correct and some are not.

Whose Are They?

In English, you can often say the same thing in several different ways. Look at the examples below:

The book belongs to Jack.
It's Jack's book.
It's his book.
It's his.

The coat belongs to me.
It's my coat.
It's mine.

Jack's **is a possessive noun. To form the possessive of a singular noun, you add an apostrophe (') and s. To form the possessive of a regular plural noun, you just add an apostrophe** *(boys')*. **For a plural noun that does not end in** *-s* **or** *-es (men, oxen)* **you add** *'s (men's, oxen's).* ***His*** **is a possessive adjective. There are two kinds:** *my, your, his, her, its, our, their;* **and** *mine, yours, his, hers, ours, theirs.* **The first group is used with a noun** *(It's their book).* **The second group is used without a noun** *(It's theirs).*

Read each of the sentences below. Then rewrite each one in different ways, using the example above as a model. The first two are done for you.

1. The ball belongs to Mary.

   It's Mary's ball.
   It's her ball.
   It's hers.

2. These coats belong to the Rays.

   They're the Rays' coats.
   They're their coats.
   They're theirs.

3. These dogs belong to Conchi.

   _____
   _____
   _____

4. The calculator belongs to me.

   _____
   _____
   _____

5. The games belong to us.

   _____
   _____
   _____

6. The cats belong to you.

   _____
   _____
   _____

7. The tape belongs to Raquel.

   _____
   _____
   _____

8. The hat belongs to Hidalgo.

   _____
   _____
   _____

9. These boots belong to Paula.

   _____
   _____
   _____

10. That bat belongs to you.

   _____
   _____
   _____

11. Those glasses belong to us.

   _____
   _____
   _____

12. The pen belongs to me.

   _____
   _____
   _____

SKILL OBJECTIVES: Forming and using possessive nouns and adjectives; restating ideas in different ways. Review/teach the formation of possessives. Draw attention to the two uses of the apostrophe. Work through the examples with the class, and show how the first item follows them. Do some or all of the remaining items orally with the class before assigning as independent written work.

3

Long, Longer, Longest

Language Objective
Complete sentences using the comparative and superlative form of adjectives.

A Place the correct form of the adjective in each sentence. Be careful of spelling changes in some of the words. Use -er or -est for short words and *more* and *the most* for longer words. The first two are done for you.

1. The Nile is (long) _____the longest_____ river in the world.

2. Alaska is (large) _____larger_____ than Texas.

3. Los Angeles is (big) _____ than Boston.

4. In 1910, England was (powerful) _____ nation in the world.

5. A Mercedes is (expensive) _____ than a Volkswagen.

6. Florida has (long) _____ coastline of all the fifty states.

7. The climate of New York is (cold) _____ than that of Miami.

8. Mount Everest is (high) _____ mountain in the world.

9. Gold is (valuable) _____ than silver.

10. Saint Augustine is (old) _____ city in the United States.

B Use the correct form of *good* or *bad* in these sentences. Use *better* or *the best* for the *good* form, and *worse* or *the worst* for the *bad* form. (Use *a* or *the* with your adjectives if you need to.) The first two are done for you.

1. Fruit is (good) _____better_____ for you than candy.

2. Many people think February is (bad) _____the worst_____ month of the year.

3. Ali feels (bad) _____ today than he did yesterday.

4. Irina speaks English (good) _____ than she writes it.

5. Lincoln was President during one of (bad) _____ periods in history.

6. The pollution in Los Angeles is (bad) _____ than the pollution in New York City.

7. The San Francisco earthquake of 1906 was (bad) _____ earthquake disaster in the history of California.

8. *Lord of the Rings* was voted (good) _____ movie of 2004.

9. Many educators believe that Harvard University is (good) _____ university in the world.

10. Route 95 is (good) _____ highway from New York to Washington than it is from Boston to New York.

C Choose appropriate adjectives to complete these sentences. Be sure your adjective makes sense in the sentence and that it is in the correct form. (Use *a* or *the* with your adjectives if you need to.)

1. Juan thought Maria was _____ girl in the world!

2. Richard has _____ stereo system than Ramona does.

3. My father thinks the Cadillac is _____ automobile.

4. Television is _____ invention of the past 100 years.

5. Sammy believes New York is _____ state than Iowa.

SKILL OBJECTIVES: Forming and using comparatives and superlatives, including those of *good*; using vocabulary in context.
Teach/review the rules for forming comparatives and superlatives. Do Part A orally; have volunteers explain their answers. Discuss the comparative and superlative forms of good, then assign the page as independent written work.

4

Cars and Houses

***The same* + a noun is one way to express a similarity.**

>   Example: Susan and Federico are *the same* age.

***The same as* is also used to express a similarity.**

>   Example: Susan's car is *the same as* John's car.

Or:

>   Susan's car is *the same* color *as* John's car.

Cars are expensive, but houses are much more expensive! Maria and Susan know this, because each of them owns a car and a house.

Ⓐ Look at the information about their cars.

Nouns	Maria's Car	Susan's Car
Color	Blue	Blue
Make	Honda	Ford
Model	Sedan	Station Wagon
Year	2004	2003
Price	$19,000	$17,500

Write some sentences comparing these two cars. The first two are done for you. Use them as models.

1. _Maria's car is the same color as Susan's car._
2. _Maria's car is_ _____
3. _____
4. _____
5. _____

Ⓑ Now look at the information about their houses.

Nouns	Maria's House	Susan's House
Value	$410,000	$560,000
Age	40 years old	10 years old
Style	Colonial	Modern
Color	White	White
Size	7 rooms	10 rooms

In your notebook, write some sentences comparing the two houses. Use nouns such as *value, age, style, color,* or *size*. Or you can use adjectives such as *old, modern, large,* or *expensive.*

SKILL OBJECTIVES: Using comparatives; interpreting data. Discuss with students that cars and houses are the two most expensive purchases that many people make. Call attention to the data on the cars, and have volunteers read the first two sentences. Do the rest of Part A orally. Discuss the information on the houses and do two sentences orally. Then assign the entire page as independent written work.

That's Superlative!

A Change each of the adjectives in the phrases at the left into its superlative form, and then use the phrase in a sentence of your own. The first one is done for you.

big city   1. _New York City is the biggest city in New York._

famous actress   2. _____

good singer   3. _____

cold state   4. _____

hot state   5. _____

tall building   6. _____

interesting personality 7. _____

good movie   8. _____

B Now write sentences that use the phrase *one of the* followed by a superlative. For example, "Boston is *one of the oldest* cities in the United States." Or, "Los Angeles is *one of the most exciting* cities in the United States." Use the phrases in the box to make your sentences.

large state	rich man	good university
long river	small state	famous movie star
beautiful city	important writer	talented rock group
popular tourist attraction		

1. _____
2. _____
3. _____
4. _____
5. _____
6. _____
7. _____
8. _____
9. _____
10. _____

C Write a paragraph about your country in your notebook. Use the phrases in the box above if you wish, or any of the following, or both. Use superlatives in your paragraph.

big city	famous athlete	good artist
important industry	beautiful view	popular musician

SKILL OBJECTIVES: Forming Sund using superlatives; writing descriptive paragraphs. *Part A:* Review the two ways of forming superlatives (with the ending *-est* and with the word *most*). Have a volunteer tell why "big city" is changed to "the biggest city" in Item 1. Do the remaining items orally, then assign as independent written work. *Part B:* Do several sentences orally, then assign as written work. Part C may be used as a homework assignment.

Similes

A A simile (SIM-uh-lee) is a way of describing something by comparing it to something else. Good writers use interesting, vivid similes to help readers form pictures in their minds.
Some similes are used over and over, however. Like old bread or cake, they become stale.
It is important to know them, just the same, because you will hear and see them so often.

The similes in Column Y are often used in conversation. **Match them with the sentence beginnings in Column X by writing the letter of the simile in the blank that follows the sentence beginning. The first one is done for you.**

X	**Y**
1. Your hands are freezing; they're ___i___	**a.** as big as a castle.
2. It's easy to pick up the baby; he's _____	**b.** as loud as thunder.
3. My brother never makes any noise, he's _____	**c.** as pretty as a picture.
4. Hurry, Juan! You're _____	**d.** as boring as yesterday's news.
5. Professor Collins's class is awfully dull. It's _____	**e.** as white as snow.
6. The gun shot rang out in the night. It was _____	**f.** as bright as stars.
7. Our new house is huge; it's _____	**g.** as old as the hills.
8. Paul would never hurt anybody; he's _____	**h.** as sweet as sugar.
9. His girlfriend is lovely; she's _____	**i.** as cold as ice.
10. Sandy can't lift the box; it's _____	**j.** as gentle as a lamb.
11. Look at the sheets and pillowcases; they're _____	**k.** as light as a feather.
12. Raoul's eyes shine; they're _____	**l.** as quiet as a mouse.
13. Everybody knows that ancient joke; it's _____	**m.** as happy as a lark.
14. Children like this medicine; it's _____	**n.** as heavy as lead.
15. Myra is very cheerful today; she's _____	**o.** as slow as a turtle.

B Now make up similes of your own. Be fresh and inventive! Some sentence beginnings are given, to get you started. Write your own for the other similes.

1. Alana's room was as colorful as _____

2. The night was as dark as _____

3. Judy's face was as red as _____

4. Shu Min is as stubborn as _____

5. The students were as curious as _____

6. _____

7. _____

8. _____

9. _____

10. _____

SKILL OBJECTIVE: Understanding and creating similes. *Part A:* Discuss the definition of a simile at the top of the page. Elicit that similes are used to help hearers or readers to understand better what we are trying to communicate. Do the first three items orally, and discuss how the similes accomplish this purpose. Assign as independent written work. *Part B:* Stress the creation of fresh, inventive similes. Ask several students to provide different answers for the first three items, then assign as written work.

In the Newspaper: the Index

Read the article.

Every large city has at least one daily newspaper. Many small cities and towns also have daily newspapers. Your daily newspaper is an important source of information. Television can give you some of the news, but a newspaper can give you more. It can "cover" (provide information about) your own area—your city or town, your state, and your country, and give you information about the rest of the world as well. It can tell you about sales in stores near you, about programs on your television channels, and about movies in your theaters. It can keep you up to date on your own sports teams, and on major

professional teams all over the nation. It can help you find a place to live, a car to buy, and a job. Get to know your newspaper! To help you, each unit in this book has pages called In the Newspaper. These will help you find out about some of the features in your own daily paper.

Most newspapers have an index. Just as the Table of Contents in a book tells you where to find each chapter, the index in a newspaper tells you where to find different kinds of information. Look at the index below. Notice that here it has a different name. In your paper it may be called something else.

Guide to Features

Arts/Films	24–25	Computer World	43–45
Bridge	42	Living Section	27–28
Business	13–15	Obituaries	38
Classified	47–62	Sports	31–33
Comics	46	TV and Radio	22–23
Editorials	16–17	Weather	10

A Match the names of the sections at the left with the kind of information that is found in them at the right by writing the correct letter in each blank. The first one is done for you.

1. Arts/Films ___d___   a. news of the stock market, banks, and companies
2. Bridge _____   b. lists of programs seen and heard in the area
3. Business _____   c. the cartoon page
4. Classified _____   d. news of movies, theater, art exhibits, concerts
5. Comics _____   e. meteorological forecasts, temperature, etc.
6. Editorials _____   f. ads for jobs, cars, houses, apartments
7. Computer World _____   g. opinions of newspaper owners, staff, and readers
8. Living Section _____   h. reports of baseball, football, hockey games
9. Obituaries _____   i. recipes, interior decorating, etiquette, advice
10. Sports _____   j. information about computer technology
11. TV and Radio _____   k. list of persons who have died recently
12. Weather _____   l. suggestions for playing a popular card game

(Go on to the next page.)

SKILL OBJECTIVES: Classifying; identifying main idea; using an index; learning about newspapers. Ask how many students read a daily newspaper regularly. What can a newspaper give them that television and radio cannot? What kinds of things can one find in a newspaper? Tell students that each unit in this book will have material on the newspaper and its parts. Then discuss the use of the newspaper's index or table of contents. *Part A:* Do the first several items orally, then assign for written work.

8

B **Use the index on the preceding page to answer the following questions. The first one is done for you.**

1. On what page would you find a story about the spring fashion shows in Paris and New York? _27_

2. Where would you look to find out about a movie that opened last night? _____

3. You're thinking about buying a used car. Where will you look in the paper? _____

4. On what page will you probably find an article about a merger of two large corporations? _____

5. You want to buy a laptop computer. Where do you look to find out about the latest models? _____

6. Your friend's grandmother just died. Where will you look to find out when her funeral is going to be? _____

7. Your city is going to elect a new mayor soon. Where do you look to find out which candidate the newspaper management is backing? _____

8. You'd like to go on a picnic tomorrow. Where will you look to see if this is a good idea or not? _____

9. You like to play cards, but sometimes you don't know what to bid. Where can you look for suggestions? _____

10. Where will you look to find out what Garfield is up to today? _____

11. Your friend has said that there are reruns of *Friends* on every day. Where will you look to see when they are on? _____

12. Your school track team is in a big meet with teams from other schools in your state. Where will you look to find out how well they succeeded yesterday? _____

C **The index on the preceding page tells you where to find some kinds of news—news about business, sports, or cultural events, for example. But it does not tell you where to find general news—news about what's happening in the Middle East or Europe or Central America, for example, or news about what the different candidates for mayor said yesterday. Think of some headings you might add to a Table of Contents to show people where to find different kinds of news. One is done for you.**

_____*National News*_____   _____

_____   _____

_____   _____

D **Get a copy of your local daily newspaper. Attach the index to the top of a sheet of paper. Then list at least one piece of information you found in each section of the paper mentioned in the Table of Contents.**

Whose Is It?

There are five mailboxes in the local post office in Boxford. The five boxes belong to five people in the town. During months of sorting mail, the postal worker has guessed certain facts about these five people. Using the fourteen pieces of information below as clues, you should be able to figure out which mailbox belongs to whom, and the occupation of each mailbox holder.

1. Richard Brady is an insurance salesman.

2. The owner of Box 3 is an electrician.

3. The banker uses an end box.

4. The teacher's name is Mr. Mahoney.

5. The box before the electrician's box belongs to Ms. Donley.

6. Frank is an electrician.

7. Susan once got Sam's mail in a mix up.

8. Box 1 belongs to the Owen family.

9. Jennifer uses Box 2.

10. The insurance salesman is next to the teacher.

11. The accountant uses Box 2.

12. The insurance salesman uses Box 5.

13. The Adlers' box is not next to the insurance salesman's box.

14. Sam's mailbox is next to Frank's.

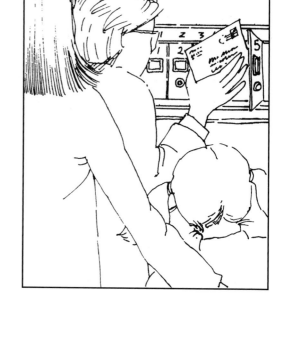

Now fill in the names and occupations of the box holders. You will have to read through the clues several times. Good luck!

	First Name	Last Name	Occupation
Box 1			
Box 2			
Box 3			
Box 4			
Box 5			

SKILL OBJECTIVES: Deductive problem solving; reading for details. Read the instructions, then draw a row of boxes on the board, numbered 1 to 5. Establish that 1 and 5 are the "end boxes." Tell students they are to find out the first and last names and occupations of the five box holders. Suggest that they draw a row of boxes like the one on the board and write clues under them as they discover them. You may wish to have students work in pairs to solve the problem.

Dear Dot

Dear Dot,
   What do girls like to do on a date? I'm not talking about going out to eat or to a movie, but before and after that. What do girls like to talk about? When I go to her house, do I have to talk to her parents? What about at the end of the date? Is a kiss on the first date all right? Anything else? I am going to be dating soon, so any information you can give me will be helpful. I don't want to look ridiculous. Thanks.
                                                    Bashful

Discuss each of the questions in class. Then write your answer.

1. Do girls and boys usually like to talk about the same things? Why or why not? _____
_____
_____

2. Does a date usually meet his girlfriend's parents? Why or why not? _____
_____
_____

3. Is a kiss on the first date all right? Why or why not? _____
_____
_____

4. Why does the writer sign himself "Bashful"? What does *bashful* mean? _____
_____
_____

Write About It

Now put yourself in Dot's place. Write a helpful answer to Bashful. Remember, you want to help him solve his problem, not make fun of him or criticize him.

   Dear Bashful,
_____
_____
_____
_____
_____

SKILL OBJECTIVES: Reading for main idea; making inferences; generalizing from experiences; expressing opinions in writing.
Read the letter aloud (or have a student read it). Discuss each question in class. Encourage free expression of opinion, but be sure students can support their opinions. Then have students write answers to the questions. Suggest that they use these answers as the basis for their letters. You may wish to assign the letter-writing activity as homework.

Language Objective
Learn to form and use adverbs.

An adverb is a word that tells *how*. Most adverbs are formed by adding *-ly* to an adjective, but some adverbs are irregular. Look at the following chart of adjectives and their adverbs.

Adjective	Adverb	Adjective	Adverb	Adjective	Adverb
careful	carefully	quick	quickly	angry	angrily
careless	carelessly	slow	slowly	good	well
polite	politely	impatient	impatiently	fast	fast
beautiful	beautifully	accurate	accurately	hard	hard

A Change the adjectives to adverbs to answer the questions. Use your dictionary if you need to. The first one is done for you.

1. Tom is a careful driver.
   How does he drive?   _He drives carefully._

2. Susan is a beautiful dancer.
   How does she dance?   _____

3. Manuel and Juan are terrible singers.
   How do they sing?   _____

4. My father is a dangerous driver.
   How does he drive?   _____

5. Carolina is a fast typist.
   How does she type?   _____

6. Carlos is a good tennis player.
   How does he play?   _____

B Look at the chart of the comparative forms of some adverbs. Use it to complete the sentences. Use each adverb only once.

better than	slower *or* more slowly than	more carefully than
worse than	louder *or* more loudly than	more quickly than
later than	neater *or* more neatly than	more beautifully than
earlier than	easier *or* more easily than	more accurately than

1. Today Juan feels _____ he did yesterday.

2. Do you speak English _____ your father does?

3. Do you dress _____ your friends?

4. Does your mother drive _____ your father?

5. Lisa works _____ her sister.

6. Do you go to bed _____ or _____ your parents?

7. I speak Spanish _____ I speak English.

8. Do you read _____ you did a year ago?

9. She does her homework _____ most students.

10. Marco often talks _____ he needs to.

SKILL OBJECTIVES: Forming and using adverbs; using the comparative form of adverbs; using context to complete sentences.
Draw attention to the definition of "adverb" and the examples showing how adverbs are formed from adjectives. Ask for other adjectives, write them on the board, and help students form the related adverbs. *Part A:* Do the items orally, then assign as written work. *Part B:* Discuss the two ways of forming comparatives, elicit when each is used, then assign the ten items as written work.

How Did They Say It?

Language Objective
Choose appropriate adverbs to complete sentences.

Read each sentence. Add an appropriate adverb from the Data Bank to complete it. Although the same adverb might be used in several sentences, you may use each adverb only once, so choose carefully.

1. "My best friend moved away last week," the boy said _____.

2. "I can't wait to get started," Paula said _____.

3. "Help me! Help me! I've been robbed!" the woman cried _____.

4. "Sshh! The baby is sleeping," the young mother said _____.

5. "I don't like to go to parties where I don't know anyone," the girl said

   _____.

6. "Darling, you are the most wonderful daughter that a father ever had," the man said

   _____.

7. "I wish I could buy that horse," said Jill _____.

8. "I'm sorry. I didn't realize that this was a private beach," the woman said

   _____.

9. "I shall never set foot in this restaurant again," the customer shouted

   _____.

10. "Are you sure that you didn't copy Roberto's exam?" the teacher asked

    _____.

11. "Well, you aren't wrong, but you're not exactly right," the counselor explained

    _____.

12. "I hate to go, but I suppose I have to," said Tony _____.

13. "I did it. I stole the five dollars," the boy admitted _____.

14. "Do you think I'll pass my driver's test?" Santiago asked _____.

15. "I just can't seem to make it come out right," the student wailed

    _____.

DATA BANK				
angrily	anxiously	apologetically	desperately	enthusiastically
helplessly	longingly	lovingly	quietly	reluctantly
sadly	shyly	suspiciously	tactfully	truthfully

SKILL OBJECTIVES: Using adverbs; building vocabulary; using context to complete sentences. Read the directions with the students. Emphasize both that more than one of the adverbs in the Data Bank may fit in a particular sentence and that the same adverb may fit several sentences; however, the student must use each adverb only once. Students may wish to "try out" answers in the margin. Students should use dictionaries for adverbs that are unfamiliar. You may wish to assign this page as homework.

13

Summing Up

A summary is a short statement of the important information contained in a paragraph, a story, or a longer reading selection. Look at the examples. Then write summaries of the other paragraphs.

Example 1

Phineas Taylor (P. T.) Barnum was the most famous showman of his time. Born in 1810, he started a kind of entertainment that is now the Ringling Brothers and Barnum & Bailey Circus.

Barnum opened his circus in 1871. He billed it as The Greatest Show on Earth. He would do or say almost anything to get people to buy tickets. Sometimes he even resorted to playing pranks on his audiences. One time he made a sign that said "To the Egress" and hung it over an opening in the tent. People thought they were going to see a strange new kind of animal and bought tickets. But Barnum fooled them. The word "egress" means the same as "exit." Even though he tricked his audiences by outrageous advertising, he did bring amazing acts to them. Jenny Lind, the Swedish Nightingale, delighted everyone with her voice and beauty. Barnum also brought Jumbo, a huge elephant—the first elephant to come to America.

Summary: _P. T. Barnum, a showman who started a new kind of entertainment, sometimes used trickery to get people to buy tickets to his shows. But he did bring some amazing acts to them._

Example 2

The Queen Elizabeth II, nicknamed the QE2, is a large, modern passenger ship. The QE2, which is actually an enormous floating hotel, can carry 2,000 passengers. A staff of 950 runs the ship and takes care of the passengers. The ship has three restaurants, four swimming pools, two movie theaters, two libraries, a hospital, and many other facilities. The QE2 made its final trans-Atlantic voyage in 2004 and now cruises the Mediterranean Sea.

Summary: _The QE2, a large ship that can carry 2,000 people, has several restaurants, swimming pools, and other facilities, and is used for passenger cruises._

Write summaries of the following passages in your notebook.

Story 1

It was one of the most exciting games of the season. In the first half, the Red Wings made two touchdowns and scored two extra points. In the second half, however, the White Sox made a comeback. "Killer" Kowalski, their quarterback, led them to three winning plays, and the Super Sox won again with a final score of 27 to 14.

Story 2

The Statue of Liberty, on Liberty Island in New York Harbor, was a gift of the people of France to the United States. It was designed by a French sculptor, Frederic Auguste Bartholdi, who began work on it in 1874. The statue arrived in America in 214 packing cases and was put together on its granite base on what was then called Bedloe's Island. The last rivet holding together the copper sheets that make up the outside of the statue was driven on October 28, 1886, when President Grover Cleveland dedicated the monument. The statue is 151 feet high, from the base to the tip of the torch. It weighs 225 tons. Between 1984 and 1986 the statue was rebuilt. The frame was repaired, the torch was replaced, and an elevator was added. The restored statue was reopened to the public at a celebration on July 4, 1986.

SKILL OBJECTIVES: Reading for main idea; writing a summary. Read the definition of a summary with the class. Have students look at the two examples. Elicit that the summaries contain the main ideas of the longer passages but omit many of the details. Ask students to write a first draft of a summary of the football game story, and have several of these read and discussed. Then assign the rest of the page. Allow time for students to complete the page, then have them work in pairs, comparing and discussing their summaries.

In Short

On the preceding page you wrote summaries of short paragraphs. More often you will be asked to write summaries of longer stories or articles. Read the article below on thoroughbred horses. Then write a summary of it.

To see a thoroughbred horse race at full speed is to witness an awesome display of strength, speed, and grace. While the history of the horse stretches back thousands of years, the existence of the thoroughbred breed goes back only 300 years or so.

The first thoroughbreds were bred in England. All horses of the thoroughbred breed are descended from what are known as the three "foundation sires." Those three horses were Darley Arabian, Byerly Turk, and Godolphin Barb. They were named for the Englishmen who brought them to Europe—Thomas Darley, Lord Godolphin, and Captain Robert Byerly. These three male horses were brought to England from the Mediterranean Middle East at different times between 1689 and 1724. Each of these stallions was either a part- or purebred Arabian horse.

Arabian horses were bred by the Bedouins, an Arab people who live a nomadic life traveling through the Middle Eastern deserts. They needed horses that were swift and brave and able to endure difficult conditions, such as running over sand and into battle. Arabian horses are known for their speed, elegant bearing, and endurance. They are known in the Arab world as "drinkers of the wind."

The horses brought to England were bred with sturdy English racing mares. The combination of the two breeds produced a strong, swift animal that could carry extra weight over distances

without tiring./They were also about eight inches taller than the Arabians. All of this was important for a growing new sport that required horses to ride competitively carrying riders and other weight: horse racing.

A racehorse's speed depends on a number of factors. Some of these are the condition of the track, how much weight the horse is carrying, and how long a distance it has to run. In addition to that, of course, individual ability and competitive spirit are vital ingredients.

Around 1730, a horse named Bulle Rock, a descendant of Darley Arabian, was imported to the United States. Bulle Rock was the first of many hundreds of thoroughbreds to be brought to the United States to begin breeding thoroughbreds in this country. Today, the breeding, care, and training of thoroughbreds is a multi-million-dollar industry.

Thoroughbreds can be almost any color. Usually they are black, gray, chestnut, or bay (reddish brown). They can be around sixteen hands (around sixty-four inches) tall and weigh between 1,000 and 1,500 pounds.

Thoroughbreds have strong lungs and powerful legs. They also have great stamina and courage. They may be somewhat high-strung and sensitive animals. While some of them participate in jumping, hunting, and polo, thoroughbreds are not used for tasks other than racing.

Write your summary below.

_____

_____

_____

_____

_____

_____

SKILL OBJECTIVES: Reading for main idea; choosing relevant details; writing a summary. Read the article. (You may wish to read it aloud to the class or have a student or students do so.) Discuss with the group what ideas should be included in a summary, and write these on the board as they are offered and agreed upon. Suggest that students copy these and use them as they write their summaries. You may wish to assign the writing of the summaries as homework.

In the Newspaper: Headlines

A A headline is the line of large print above a newspaper article. It calls attention to the article and usually gives the main idea. Read the following articles. Then look at the four headlines in the box below and write each one above the article it goes with.

A long-abandoned mansion on Long Island where Marilyn Monroe once lived has burned to the ground. Suffolk County police believe the fire may have been set deliberately.

The former Chandler estate had no electricity or other power, leading investigators to consider arson. More than 200 volunteer firefighters worked for over three hours to put the fire out.

The Chandler family purchased the mansion and surrounding property in the 1940s. Marilyn Monroe and her then-husband Arthur Miller were among many artists, writers, and actors who rented the mansion from the Chandlers in the 1960s.

A hungry moose carried off a Swedish couple's bicycle last Monday, the couple said.

Bjorn and Monica Helamb, whose rose garden has been a yearly food target for the moose, had placed the bicycle there, hoping to hinder the moose's munching. But "Droopy"—so named because of its floppy ears—merely slid its head through the bike frame and started chewing. After it finished, the animal walked off with the bike still around its neck.

The bike was later found, bent beyond repair, about 1,600 feet from the couple's home.

A 22-year-old Connecticut student has become the youngest person to climb the highest peaks on each of the seven continents, the Associated Press said. In topping Mt. Everest in Nepal last Monday, Britton Keeshan of Greenwich broke the record set by Atsushi Yamada of Japan, who was 23 when he did it two years ago.

Keeshan, the grandson of the late Bob "Captain Kangaroo" Keeshan of TV fame, is one of only 33 Americans and fewer than a total of 100 people to have climbed the seven peaks— Mt. Everest, Mt. Aconcagua (Argentina), Mt. McKinley (Alaska), Mt. Kilimanjaro (Tanzania), Mt. Elbrus (on the Georgia-Russia border), Mt. Vinson Massif (Antarctica), and Mt. Kosciusko (Australia).

A retired New York City police official and veteran narcotics detective has been chosen to serve as the next chief of police of Hartford, CT, Hartford Mayor Eddie Perez announced today. Patrick J. Hartnett, 61, will replace interim Chief Mark Pawlina, who took over when former Chief Bruce Marquis resigned in January. This is Perez's first major appointment since assuming enhanced powers this year under a revised city charter.

A native New Yorker, Hartnett served as head of the NYPD Narcotics Division during the 1990s. After his retirement a few years ago, Hartnett started his own law-enforcement consulting firm.

Swedish Moose is a Bike Thief	**Celebrity Mansion Goes Up in Smoke**
CT Student Scales Seven Peaks	**Hartford Picks NY Vet for Top Cop**

B Write other headlines for these same stories in your notebook. Keep your headlines to no more than two lines of 18 characters (letters and spaces) each (total: 36 characters).

(Go on to the next page.)

SKILL OBJECTIVES: Reading for main idea; writing headlines; learning about newspapers. Discuss why headlines are used. Elicit that they tell the main idea of an article and also help the reader decide whether to read the story. Part A: Have a student read the first article aloud, then have the class decide which headline fits it. Do the other articles independently. Part B: Elicit that these articles could have different headlines, and encourage students to write new ones for each article.

C Now write headlines for the following articles.

More than 2,000 people in the Dominican Republic and Haiti have been reported dead in the wake of the heavy rains that caused the Solie River in the Dominican border town of Jimani to overflow its banks three days ago. Hundreds are still missing, the Associated Press said today.

In the Dominican Republic, about 450 homes were completely flooded, and at least fourteen small towns have lost phone service and electric power.

Troops from a U.S.-led multinational coalition had been in Haiti to stabilize the country after President Jean-Bertrand Aristide was ousted two months ago. The troops were then dispatched to assorted Haitian towns with drinking water, medical supplies, and food.

The floods are the deadliest natural disaster to have struck the area in recent memory. In 1994, Tropical Storm Gordon caused mudslides in which at least 829 Haitians died. Last September, about thirty people died in floods caused by heavy rains in St. Marc, about 45 miles northwest of the Haitian capital, Port-au-Prince.

A Russian research scientist has died after accidentally sticking herself with a needle containing the Ebola virus, according to the scientist's research center.

Antonina Prenyakova was conducting Ebola research on May 5, said Natalia Pinskaya, a spokeswoman for the Vektor State Research Center of Virology and Biotechnology outside Novosibirsk in central Siberia, when the mishap occurred. Pinskaya said that all efforts to treat Prenyakova had failed, and that all research workers and medical personnel who had been in contact with the victim would remain under observation for three weeks. There is no current vaccine or remedy for Ebola, which is spread by contact with body fluids, including sweat and saliva.

The incident was the third time a worker at the facility, which had operated as a biological weapons lab during the Soviet era, had accidentally contracted a deadly virus.

D Clip several articles from your own newspaper. Cut off the headlines, and exchange the articles with classmates. Write headlines for the articles. Then compare them with the headlines that appeared in the newspaper. Do your headlines give a correct idea of the article? Do they call attention to it? Do they present its main idea? Are they as successful in doing these things as those that appeared in the newspaper? Discuss with the class some of the problems in writing headlines.

E Headlines are not always clear when read out of context. Look at these headlines. Then write in your notebook, or discuss with classmates, what each article was probably about. Use your dictionary for words you don't know.

1. Van Could Take Pix in Motion

2. Old Man River Runneth Over

3. Jobless Rate at 10-Year Low

4. Coach Asks Subs to Take a Leap

5. Rose Cites Cost as Business Ends

6. Pistons Stifle Stars Once More

7. Market Surges to New High

8. Car Alarms to Disappear Soon

9. Dow Surges On Third Day in Row

10. Speeding Celeb Caught on Camera

Read All About It

All newspapers use headlines to attract attention. Some writers use sensational headlines to trick people into buying worthless newspapers. The stories that follow these sensational headlines usually turn out to be silly or untrue. Look at the headlines below. Decide which ones would be likely to appear in a serious newspaper and which are sensational or silly. Label each headline *Serious* or *Silly* on the line under it. The first one is done for you.

1. Bigfoot Lives, Woman Claims

   _____ Silly _____

2. 200 Killed in Plane Crash

   _____

3. 36 Homeless in Apartment Fire

   _____

4. Aliens Took Me to Their Home on Mars

   _____

5. Millionaire Leaves Fortune to Pet Cat

   _____

6. 50,000 New Cars Recalled for Possible Brake Defect

   _____

7. Three Ghosts Live in My Basement, Says Film Star

   _____

8. Guilty Verdict for Man in Killing of Wife, 2 Kids

   _____

9. 108 Dogs Not Enough, Family Wants More

   _____

10. Hurricane Causes $6 Million Damage

    _____

11. Girl Can Read at Three Months

    _____

12. Thousands Drive to Work as Train Workers Strike

    _____

13. Husband and Wife Offer to Trade Baby for New Car

    _____

14. Hijackers Take Plane, Hold 387 People Hostage

    _____

15. Famine Hits Angola, Thousands Starving

    _____

16. Psychic Predicts Queen to Marry Rock Singer

    _____

17. Anger Mounts as Strike at Bradley Auto Enters 12th Week

    _____

18. Woman Loses 15 Pounds in 2 Days with Wonder Diet

    _____

SKILL OBJECTIVES: Making judgments; categorizing; expanding vocabulary. Read the paragraph at the top of the page orally to the students. Discuss headlines and the kind of tabloid often found in supermarkets. Ask students which newspaper(s) they read. Have they ever read any of the sensational tabloids? Which? Where? When students understand the concept of serious and silly headlines, assign the page for independent work. Review as a group, having students take turns reading headlines and giving their answers; have them explain why they chose one category rather than the other.

Adjective or Adverb?

Language Objectives
Choose the correct adjective or adverb form to complete a sentence. Write sentences for adjective and adverb cues.

Adjectives describe or tell about nouns or pronouns. Look at the examples:

Ann's a *pretty* girl.   My nightmare was *awful*!   That's a *wild* animal.

Adverbs describe or tell about verbs and adjectives. Look at the examples:

She ran *quickly*.   It's *extremely* hot.   She spoke too *slowly*.

A **Look at the sentences below. Decide whether the adjective or the adverb completes the sentence best. Circle your answer. The first one is done for you.**

1. He ran (quick / quickly) down the street.

2. My (sad / sadly) friend doesn't like to talk about his problems.

3. Everyone watched the (horrible / horribly) accident in silence.

4. That movie was (amazing / amazingly).

5. I breathed (rapid / rapidly) after I ran up all those steps.

6. Oswaldo is (extreme / extremely) interested in bicycles.

7. Gloria is (awful / awfully) old to be playing with dolls, isn't she?

8. I don't understand algebra very (good / well).

9. That is one of the most (peaceful / peacefully) countries in the world.

10. Those (brave / bravely) soldiers received medals for their actions.

11. The ocean waves slapped (loud / loudly) against the rocks.

12. Yoshiko tiptoed out of the baby's room (quiet / quietly).

13. That house is too (expensive / expensively) for us.

14. I thought those paintings were (incredible / incredibly) ugly.

15. Everyone is (hungry / hungrily) for supper.

16. The students behaved (bad / badly) when their teacher was away.

17. She spoke (insolent / insolently) to her parents.

18. The children waited (hungry / hungrily) for their lunch.

19. I listened (patient / patiently) to the policeman's warning.

20. I can't go; I'm (terrible / terribly) sick.

B **Now write a sentence in your notebook for each of the following words. Make sure you use the adjectives as adjectives and the adverbs as adverbs.**

serious	strange	nervous	beautiful	recent
seriously	strangely	nervously	beautifully	recently

SKILL OBJECTIVES: Choosing between adjectives and adverbs; building vocabulary; internalizing grammar rules. Review the boxed explanation of adjectives and adverbs at the top of the page. Make sure that students understand the concept of nouns, pronouns, and verbs as well as adjectives and adverbs. Do a few examples as a class, then assign students time to complete the page on their own. Review the page together, with students reading the complete sentences aloud. Have students explain their choices.

Dear Dot

Dear Dot,

How can I make friends? I am new in town, and I don't have any friends here yet. Before I came here, I had lots of friends, but they were the people I grew up with. They were always my friends. I don't remember getting to know them, they were just always there from the first grade. I have been here for six weeks now, and some of the kids are starting to smile and say hello, but I don't really have any friends yet. What can I do?

Lonely

Discuss each of the questions in class. Then write your answers.

1. Do most people have this problem when they move? Why or why not? _____

_____

_____

2. What are some good places to make new friends? _____

_____

_____

3. How should a person act when he or she is trying to make new friends? _____

_____

_____

4. How long does it usually take to make new friends? _____

_____

_____

5. Are the first people you meet always likely to become good friends? Why or why not?

_____

_____

Write About It

Now put yourself in Dot's place. Write a helpful answer to Lonely. Remember, you want to help solve the problem, not make fun of the writer or criticize.

Dear Lonely,

_____

_____

_____

_____

_____

SKILL OBJECTIVES: Reading for main idea; making inferences; generalizing from experience; expressing opinions in writing.
Have students read the letter. Discuss each question in class. Encourage free expression of opinion, but be sure students can support their opinions. Then have students write answers to the questions. Suggest that they use these answers as the basis for their letters. You may wish to assign the letter-writing activity as homework.

20

Language Objective
Restate time implications
of verb tenses.

In English, one statement often *implies* or *includes* another idea. Look at the example below. Read the sentence in boldface type. Then look at the three sentences under it. Which one is implied by the boldfaced sentence? In other words, which one *has to* be true if the boldfaced sentence is true?

Example: Karl has been an engineer for five years.

a. He's an engineer now.

b. He was an engineer, but he isn't one now.

c. He is going to be an engineer.

You should have chosen *a*. The structure "has been ... for" implies an action or a condition that started in the past and is still going on. If Karl has been an engineer for five years, he is still an engineer, so *a* is correct.

A Now look at each of the items below. Choose the answer that is implied by the statement and circle it.

1. Kathy has already taken a shower.

a. She is going to take a shower.

b. She took a shower.

c. She takes a shower every morning.

2. Paul has worked at the bank for ten years.

a. He is going to work at the bank.

b. He works at the bank.

c. He doesn't work at the bank anymore.

3. Carla and Roberto have been students for seven years.

a. They plan to study in the future.

b. They studied seven years ago and stopped studying.

c. They are students.

4. I have seen the movie *The Matrix* six times.

a. I saw the movie.

b. I'm going to see the movie.

c. I want to see the movie.

5. You have lived in the United States for three years.

a. You came to the United States three years ago.

b. You plan to live in the United States three years from now.

c. You have come to the United States three times.

6. Jesús has been in the hospital for a week.

a. He was in the hospital, but he isn't there now.

b. He is going to go to the hospital.

c. He's in the hospital now.

B Circle the correct answers to the questions.

1. When you saw John, what was he doing?

a. He played soccer.

b. He was playing soccer.

c. He plays soccer.

2. Has Sunita ever broken her leg?

a. Yes, she did.

b. Yes, she was.

c. Yes, she has.

SKILL OBJECTIVES: Using present perfect tense; using time expressions with *for*; understanding implied meaning. Teach/review the present perfect tense. Discuss implied meanings. Be sure students understand that a meaning can be implied without being specifically stated. Do the example; have a volunteer explain why *a* is correct. *Part A:* Do several items orally, discussing each one, then assign as written work. *Part B:* Do the first item orally, discuss why *b* is correct, then assign the second item as written work.

Erek and Ilya

Rewrite the following paragraphs using the correct form of the verb in parentheses. Use only the simple past (*ate*) or the present perfect (*has eaten*).

Language Objective
Distinguish between the simple past and the present perfect tense while rewriting a passage.

Erek and Ilya (come) to the United States three years ago. When they first (start) school, they (be) very nervous because they (not speak) any English. Now they speak English very well, of course, because they (live) here for three years and (study) the language.

After school, Ilya works at a small grocery store near her apartment. She (work) at the store for eight months. Last month, she (work) there two afternoons a week, but now she works three afternoons a week.

Erek doesn't work after school because when he finishes his homework, he teaches English to his aunt and uncle who (arrive) from Poland three months ago. In the past month, his aunt and uncle (learn) 200 new words, and Erek (already teach) them the past tense. When Erek first (begin) teaching them, he (not have) much patience, but now he feels more comfortable. As a matter of fact, he (already decide) that when he graduates from high school, he wants to go to college and study education.

Ilya's father is from Russia and her mother is from Ukraine. Her parents first (meet) in Brooklyn, New York, when they (be) visiting relatives. Several years later, they (get) married. They (live) in Moscow for many years before they (move) to Brooklyn three years ago.

SKILL OBJECTIVES: Choosing between simple past and present perfect tense; using context to determine correct tense. Read the instructions with the class. Emphasize that they must use only the simple past or present perfect tense of the verb in parentheses. Do the first paragraph orally. Then perhaps assign the page as homework. Be sure students understand they are to rewrite the entire story. They may use more paper if necessary. After they are done, discuss the final paragraph. Make sure they understand why the first four verbs should be simple past and the last two should be present perfect before reviewing the use of the rest of the verbs in that paragraph.

The Past Perfect

Read these rules about forming and using the past perfect tense.

Language Objective
Use rules to help you form and use the past perfect tense.

The past perfect tense is formed with *had* and the past participle.

I had seen	We had seen
You had seen	You had seen
He had seen	
She had seen	They had seen
It had seen	

The past perfect tense describes an action that took place in the past before another past action.

Example: Yesterday   8:00   9:00
                                  I wrote a letter   I mailed the letter

I *mailed* the letter after I *had written* it.

A   **Use the past perfect tense in the following sentences. The first one is done for you.**

1. When I arrived at the bus station, the bus (leave) _had left._

2. The bank (close) _____ five minutes before I got there.

3. When we got to the theater, the movie (start) _____.

4. Mrs. Jones called the doctor because her son (eat) _____ twenty aspirin.

5. Before I took the test, I (study) _____ for it.

B   **Combine the following sentences into one sentence. Use the simple past and the past perfect tense.**

Example:

First, I did my homework.   _After I had done my homework, I watched television._
Then I watched television.   _(or) I watched television after I had done my homework._

1. First, I washed the dishes.
    Then I dried them.

1. _____

2. First, I took a bath.
    Then I got dressed.

2. _____

3. First, I cooked dinner.
    Then I ate it.

3. _____

4. First, I took out a loan.
    Then I bought the car.

4. _____

5. First, I got on the bus.
    Then I paid my fare.

5. _____

SKILL OBJECTIVES: Forming and using the past perfect tense; combining sentences using *after*. Teach/review the formation of the past perfect tense. Do the example; be sure students understand the relation between the two past actions. Ask for other examples and put them on the board. *Part A:* Discuss the first item, then assign as independent written work. *Part B:* Point out the two ways of combining the sentences; tell students they may use either. Do the first item orally, then assign as written work.

Just the Facts

Look at the pictures.

Language Objective
Use the simple past and past perfect tenses to describe a robbery.

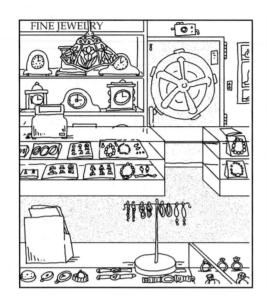 

Last night, somebody broke into a jewelry store. What did the robber do? The first two answers are done for you.

1. _The robber broke into the safe._

2. _The robber stole the jewelry in the safe._

3. _____

4. _____

5. _____

6. _____

When the owner got to her store the next morning, she saw what the robber had done. She called the police and reported the theft. What did the store owner say to the police? The first two answers are done for you.

1. _The owner said that someone had broken into the store._

2. _The robber had broken into the safe._

3. _____

4. _____

5. _____

6. _____

SKILL OBJECTIVES: Using the simple past and past perfect tenses; understanding and using reported speech. Elicit that the pictures show a jewelry store before and after a break-in. Tell the students to use the pictures to answer "What did the robber do?" Discuss several answers; elicit why the simple past tense is used. Point out that the second part of the page asks, "What did the store owner say?" Discuss why the past perfect tense is used for reported speech. Do several items orally, then assign as independent written work.

What the Puzzler Has Done

Language Objective
Solve a crossword puzzle using past participles.

Write the words in the right places. Numbers 1 Across and 1 Down are done for you.

Across

1. What the ship has done.
4. What the professor has done.
6. What the listener has done.
8. What the novelist has done.
13. What the sad man has done.
14. What the successful student has done.
17. What the girl who has read page 1 has done.
18. What the finders have done.
20. What the lecturer has done.
21. What the eyes have done.
24. What the story teller has done.
25. What the hands have done.
27. What the words have done.
28. What the thief has done.
29. What the miners have done.

Down

1. What the soprano has done.
2. What the successful test taker has done.
3. What the receivers of gifts have done.
4. What the paper shredder has done.
5. What the philosophers have done.
7. What the bells have done.
9. What the diners have done.
10. What the pilot has done.
11. What the thirsty children have done.
12. What the careless waiters have done.
15. What the artists have done.
16. What the dreamers have done.
17. What the mail carrier has done.
19. What the baseball player has done.
20. What the speaker has done.
21. What the swimmers have done.
22. What the new neighbors have done.
23. What the people in chairs have done.
26. What the team's captain has done.

(Answers are on page 117.)

SKILL OBJECTIVES: Reviewing the present perfect tense; using past participles. Do the first few Across and Down clues with the class. Be sure students understand how to fill in a crossword puzzle; elicit the way in which the Across and Down answers interlock. Tell students they may check spelling with a dictionary. You may wish to assign the puzzle as homework or have students work on it in pairs.

In the Newspaper: Examining a News Article

Language Objectives
Answer questions about a reading. Write a news article.

A news article is a report of something that happened.
A good news article tells what happened, whom it happened to, when it happened, where it happened, and sometimes why it happened.

Because people are busy, and because there are many articles in each issue of a newspaper, reporters try to put the "what, who, when, where, and why" (*w's*) into the first or "lead" paragraph. This gives busy readers the basic facts. If they want to find out more about the happening, they can read the rest of the story.

A Read the two articles below. Both tell about the same event. Which one includes the important *w's* in its lead paragraph? After you have read the articles, answer the questions about them.

Article A

POLICE NAB NEWARK MAN FOR EIGHT BANK ROBBERIES

by Rollo Bills

A Newark man has been arrested and charged with eight bank robberies committed in Essex and Union counties within the past three weeks, police say. Graham R. Charles, 44, was arrested Thursday morning in an Irvington motel.

Officers from the Nutley Police Department were led to the motel by an anonymous caller. There, they arrested Charles and a female companion, Maureen B. Hanlon, 26, when the two were found in possession of weapons. Further investigation led the police to charge Charles in the bank robberies. The arrests came a day after the FBI had released photos of the robbery suspect, which had come off security cameras posted in a number of the banks.

In each case, the robber had given bank tellers handwritten notes demanding $50 and $100 bills. No weapon was ever shown. The robberies occurred at Valley National Bank in Belleville; Valley National's Union branch; Provident Bank in Bloomfield, and Valley National Bank in Newark; Fleet Bank's Irvington branch; its Union branch; its Rahway branch; and Valley National's Nutley branch— all between May 6 and May 25.

According to Nutley Police Chief Ronald Amsterdam, the suspect's picture had been posted at one of the banks he is accused of robbing. "When he walked in the door, his photo was on the wall. . . . He walked past his own picture," Amsterdam told the *Jersey City News*.

Article B

CHARGE MADE IN EIGHT JERSEY BANK ROBBERIES; NEWARK MAN HELD

by Rollo Bills

A Newark man who brazenly walked past a picture of himself posted at the entrance to a bank has been charged with a string of bank robberies that have plagued Essex and Union counties over the past three weeks.

The suspect, Graham R. Charles, 44, was arrested Thursday morning in an Irvington motel. Nutley Police say he answered a knock at the door holding a pipe in one hand. Police then arrested Charles and his companion, Maureen B. Hanlon, 26, on a weapons possession charge. Later investigation prompted police to charge Charles in the bank robberies.

In each of the robberies, the suspect had given handwritten notes to bank tellers, demanding $50 and $100 bills. No weapon was ever shown, however. All eight robberies occurred between May 6 and 25.

Ronald Amsterdam, the Nutley police chief, said that an anonymous phone call had come in to the department around 8:15 a.m. Thursday with information as to Charles' whereabouts. The arrest came one day after the FBI had posted photos of the suspect that had been taken from various bank security cameras.

One of these photos was posted inside a bank that Charles is accused of robbing. "When he walked in the door, his photo was on the wall," Amsterdam told the *Jersey City News*, shaking his head at the suspect's gall. "He walked past his own picture."

(Go on to the next page.)

SKILL OBJECTIVES: Organizing information; understanding news articles; identifying reported speech and direct quotations.
Discuss the characteristics of a news article and the reasons for putting the basic facts into the first or "lead" paragraph. Have volunteers read the two articles aloud, and have the class compare and discuss them. Call attention to the use of reported speech, and elicit that the past perfect tense is used. Point out that both articles also use direct quotations, identified by quotation marks.

1. Which article includes the five *w*'s in the first paragraph? Circle your answer.

               Article A   Article B

2. What is the main idea of the articles? Circle the correct letter.
   a. Anonymous tips sometimes help solve crimes.
   b. A man was arrested and charged in a series of bank robberies.
   c. You can rob banks even if you do not show a weapon.
   d. New Jersey banks are not safe places to put your money.

3. What was Charles holding when he answered the door?

   _____

4. Name two of the banks that Charles was accused of robbing.

   _____

5. The articles include a "byline." Where does it come in the article? What does it tell? Why is it called a byline? (You may need to use your dictionary.)

   _____

   _____

6. Which headline do you think is the better one? Give two reasons why.

   _____

   _____

B **News articles are written in an "inverted pyramid" form. As you have seen, this means that the most important facts in the article come in the first paragraph. Less important facts come in the later paragraphs. This form makes it possible for a reader to find out quickly what the article is about. It also makes it possible for an editor to cut the story easily to make it fit the available space. The editor can do this simply by removing paragraphs from the end of the story.**

In your notebook, write a news article of your own. Use the following facts:

1. The team general manager called a press conference.

2. The conference was at 11:00 a.m. yesterday.

3. The conference was to announce that the team had just signed Sluggo Lebowski, the most feared hitter in baseball.

4. Lebowski spoke at the press conference. He said, "It is a childhood dream come true to be able to play for this team." He said that he was grateful to his agent for working out the deal with the team and that he hoped that the team would be competing for the world championship in the World Series in September.

5. Since the signing was announced, ticket sales have shot up 80 percent at the team's home stadium.

6. Lebowski will be wearing Number 32 on his uniform.

Add other facts if you wish. Do not put in your own opinion, however. A news article is a report of what happened, not a place to comment on it. It is all right to report other peoples' opinions—they are news. But the reporter's opinions should be omitted from a news article. (Other kinds of articles—columns, editorials, "feature" articles—can include the writer's opinions, however.)

SKILL OBJECTIVES: Reading for main idea and details; organizing information; making judgments; writing news articles.
Part A: Do the questions orally with the class, then assign as independent written work. *Part B:* Discuss the concept of the "inverted pyramid." Elicit that the news-article structure can be helpful in writing any kind of report. Call attention to the need for objectivity in news articles, and discuss the other kinds of writing found in newspapers in which opinion is acceptable or desirable.

Preparing for Tests: Inferences and Conclusions

Read the article.

Paul Bunyan is a well-known American folk hero. The origins of his legend are unclear. Some folklore experts say the tale was started by the French Canadians. Others say the tale originated with a Western logging company during the early twentieth century. Still others say the story character came from Europe. No one really knows exactly where this bigger-than-life tall tale started.

Paul Bunyan stories were told by lumberjacks and loggers in the Northwoods of Minnesota. As the stories were repeated, they became more and more fantastic.

Paul Bunyan was very unusual. The stories about him say that he weighed 80 pounds when he was born, and five storks were needed to deliver him to his parents. After one week, he was big enough to wear his father's clothes. His baby carriage was a lumber wagon that was pulled by a team of oxen.

Later on, the stories say, Paul had an ox—Babe, the Big Blue Ox. Babe was so big, it was said, that it took a crow one whole day to fly from one of Babe's horns to the other.

Paul's fellow lumberjacks were known as the Seven Axemen. Each of the Axemen was over six feet tall and weighed over 350 pounds. They worked together, swinging their axe blades on rope handles like a giant circular saw.

Circle the best answer for each question.

1. Who was Paul Bunyan?
  a. a foot doctor   **b.** a folk hero   **c.** a famous athlete   **d.** a cattle wrangler

2. It may be inferred from the selection that Paul Bunyan was a giant because he
  a. was European.   **b.** weighed 80 pounds at birth.   **c.** was thin.   **d.** had an ox.

3. It can be concluded that the Seven Axemen were
  a. brothers.   **b.** easy to work with.   **c.** friendly.   **d.** as fictional as Paul Bunyan.

4. Which of the following does not belong with the others?
  a. tall tale
  b. lumberjack
  c. axe
  d. logging

5. The author indicates that
  a. Paul Bunyan was an ox.
  b. any tall tale has to be at least 1,000 years old.
  c. no one is sure where the legend of Paul Bunyan got started.
  d. the French Canadians invented Babe.

SKILL OBJECTIVES: Reading for inference; finding specific information; drawing conclusions. Explain to students that this exercise is typical of reading items on standardized tests. Explain the importance of reading carefully but quickly. You may want to time the students, so that they get used to pacing themselves on a reading passage and its associated questions. (Six minutes is the suggested time limit for this on some standardized tests.) After students have completed the page, reread the passage orally, and have students tell you their answers to the questions. Discuss/explain all answers, paying special attention to inference questions.

Dear Dot

Dear Dot,

I'm fifteen years old. I do very well in school, and I work part-time three days a week. After I finish my homework, I like to watch television, but my parents insist that I need my rest, and I have to be in bed by 10:00. I think I'm old enough to decide my own bedtime. I think I have shown my parents that I am responsible by getting good grades and holding a job. How else can I convince them to let me make my own decisions in this matter?

Paulette

Discuss each of the questions in class. Then write your answers.

1. Do parents have the right to control TV watching and bedtime hours? Why or why not?

_____

2. When do children become responsible for themselves? Give reasons for your answer.

_____

_____

3. Is Paulette responsible? Why or why not? _____

_____

4. How can Paulette change her parents' minds? _____

_____

Write About It

Now put yourself in Dot's place. Write a helpful answer to Paulette. Remember, you want to help her solve her problem, not to make fun of her or criticize her.

Dear Paulette, _____

_____

_____

_____

_____

_____

SKILL OBJECTIVES: Reading for main idea, making inferences; making judgments; expressing opinions in writing. Have students read the letter. Discuss each question in class. Encourage free expression of opinion, but be sure students can support their opinions. Then have students write answers to the questions. Suggest that they use these answers as the basis for their letters. You may wish to assign the letter-writing activity as homework.

Unit 4 Tag Endings

It's Up to You, Isn't It?

Language Objectives
Ask questions with tag endings. Interview people to collect information.

A "tag ending" is a short question that follows a statement. It asks the listener to agree or disagree with the statement, to confirm it or deny it. A tag ending (or tag question) can be answered with a simple *yes* or *no* or it can be answered with a longer statement. To find the verb to use in the tag ending, in your mind change a positive statement to a negative question. "You opened the window" becomes "Didn't you open the window?" The statement with its tag ending then is "You opened the window, *didn't you*?" Look at the examples:

The traffic is heavy today, *isn't it?*

You watched the football game on TV, *didn't you?*

A Add tag endings to these statements. Look at the tense of the verb and then decide what the tag ending should be.

1. Lisa can drive a car, _____?

2. You'll be back before noon, _____?

3. Jim is coming to my party, _____?

4. I should read the directions before taking the medicine, _____?

5. You were absent from school yesterday, _____?

6. We had a lot of homework last night, _____?

7. Susan will graduate in June, _____?

8. She's already done her homework, _____?

9. It was hot yesterday, _____?

10. The bus comes at 10:15, _____?

11. It takes five hours to fly to New York, _____?

12. He has been working at the bank for a long time, _____?

Now add tag endings to these statements, then ask the questions to two students in your class. Ask the students to answer *yes* or *no*. Record your answers.

	Student 1	Student 2
1. You're from China, _____?		
2. You live in Boston, _____?		
3. You have a driver's license, _____?		
4. You did your English homework, _____?		
5. You were fifteen last year, _____?		
6. You will graduate next year, _____?		
7. You play volleyball, _____?		
8. You saw the movie *Gladiator*, _____?		
9. You've been in the U.S. for a year, _____?		
10. You can swim, _____?		

SKILL OBJECTIVES: Forming Tag using tag endings; asking and answering questions; plotting information on charts. Read the introductory paragraph with the class. Be sure students understand how to form tag endings. *Part A:* Do the items orally, then assign as independent written work. *Part B:* Have volunteers give tag endings for the first three items. Then have students complete the tag endings independently and ask and record answers to the questions. Later, have students report their results to the class.

What Do You Know?

Test yourself. Make the following statements into questions by adding tag endings. Then answer the questions. Use the Internet, an encyclopedia, or an atlas if you need to.

A Use a negative tag ending with a positive statement. The first two are done for you. Use them as models.

1. The capital of California is San Francisco, _isn't it?_

   No, it's Sacramento.

2. New Hampshire has a short coastline, _doesn't it?_

   Yes, it does.

3. Alaska is the largest state, _____?

   _____

4. People from Sweden are Swiss, _____?

   _____

5. The Dominican Republic and Haiti share the same island, _____?

   _____

6. Much of the world's diamonds comes from South Africa, _____?

   _____

7. The official languages of Canada are English and Spanish, _____?

   _____

B Use an affirmative tag ending with a negative statement. The first two are done for you. Use them as models.

1. Lima isn't the capital of Peru, _is it?_

   Yes, it is.

2. Kangaroos don't live in Austria, _do they?_

   No, they live in Australia.

3. Australia isn't a continent, _____?

   _____

4. Saudi Arabia doesn't export oil, _____?

   _____

5. People in Switzerland don't speak Dutch, _____?

   _____

6. Brazilians aren't very fond of coffee, _____?

   _____

7. The Pacific isn't the largest ocean, _____?

   _____

SKILL OBJECTIVES: Forming and using tag endings; using reference materials; building knowledge of world geography. Review the formation of tag endings; remind students that positive statements take negative tag questions, and point out that negative statements take positive tag questions. Stress that students are not expected to know the answers to many of the items on the page but are to use the Internet, an encyclopedia, or an atlas. Do the examples for each part with the class before assigning that part as independent written work.

31

Voting: the Power of Adult Citizens

Read the article.

Language Objectives
Answer questions about a reading. Write an expository paragraph that supports a topic statement.

One of the basic principles of the United States government is *popular sovereignty.* *Popular* means "of the people." *Sovereignty* means "rule" or "power." So the government is based on the idea that the people are the rulers. They hold all the power. The United States is a republic. The word *republic* means "a government in which supreme power resides in a body of citizens entitled to vote and is exercised by elected officers and representatives responsible to them and governing according to law."

The people use this power when they vote. The people vote for the president and vice president every four years. The people vote for senators every six years and members of the House of Representatives every two years. The people also vote for members of their state legislature (the people that make state laws), their state governor, and for many other officials in their state, county, and city or town.

Not everyone who lives in the United States has the right to vote. To vote, a person has to be a citizen, and has to be at least 18 years old. To vote, he or she has to register. (In North Dakota and in parts of some other states, this is not necessary.) The person has to prove that he or she is a citizen of the United States and a resident of the state in which he or she will vote.

Voting is done in several ways. In some areas, the voter is given a *ballot,* a piece of paper with the names of the different candidates for each office printed on it. The voter marks an "X" next to the names of the candidates he or she prefers.

In other areas, voting is done by machine. The voter moves a lever down under the names of the candidates he or she is voting for. After all choices are made, the voter pulls another lever to record the vote.

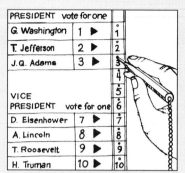

Punch card method

Some areas may use a punch-card method. The voter punches holes next to the names of the chosen candidates. After everyone has voted, the cards are put into a computer that counts the number of holes punched for each candidate.

In all these methods, the voter's choice is *secret.* No one but the voter knows how he or she voted. A voter may tell, but no one can make him or her reveal that information.

Since 1971, nearly all citizens over 18 can vote. But this was not always true. When the Constitution was adopted in 1789, no state allowed women to vote. In many states, a man had to own property or belong to a particular church. Slaves could not vote. No one under 21 could vote. Gradually, these limits on voting rights were eliminated. African-American men gained the right to vote in 1870, but some states set up rules that made it almost impossible for many of them to vote. And absolutely no women could vote. A few states allowed women to vote starting in 1869, but not until 1920 could all American women vote. The Civil Rights protests in the 1960s caused voting reforms, and now, except for certain criminals and people in mental hospitals, all citizens over the age of 18 have the right to vote.

(Go on to the next page.)

A Refer to the article on voting on the previous page. Read the statements below. If the statement is true, write *T*. If the statement is false, write *F*. If the story doesn't give you enough information to know if the statement is true or false, write *?*. The first two are done for you.

1. Popular sovereignty means that the people hold the power.   <u> T </u>

2. Voters always vote in every election.   <u> ? </u>

3. Americans elect a new president every four years.   <u>   </u>

4. Americans elect members of the Senate and House of Representatives every four years.   <u>   </u>

5. Senators and representatives make laws.   <u>   </u>

6. Americans elect governors every four years.   <u>   </u>

7. A governor is the highest state official.   <u>   </u>

8. You must be a resident of the state for one year to vote.   <u>   </u>

9. The voter's choice is always secret.   <u>   </u>

10. People usually vote in schools or government buildings.   <u>   </u>

11. African-American men had the right to vote after 1870.   <u>   </u>

12. People in mental hospitals can vote.   <u>   </u>

13. No women could vote until 1920.   <u>   </u>

14. You should know as much as you can about the person you vote for.   <u>   </u>

B You read in the article that, in 1971, the voting age was reduced from 21 to 18. Before that year, the voting age was 21 in most states. Are 18-year-olds mature enough to vote? Decide how you feel about the issue and then write an essay supporting your decision. Use your notebook if you need to.

_____

_____

_____

_____

_____

_____

_____

_____

_____

_____

SKILL OBJECTIVES: Reading for details; supporting opinions in writing. *Part A:* Review the *True, False, ?* format. Emphasize that if the article does not provide information for the answer, the question mark must be used, even if the student knows from other sources that the sentence is true or false. *Part B:* Read the instructions orally and discuss the question with the class. You may wish to have students write their essays as homework.

And So Do I

Two sentences describing the same action can be combined into one sentence in several ways. Look at the examples below:

Aramienta missed the bus. Fred missed the bus.

a. Aramienta missed the bus, and Fred did, too.

b. Aramienta missed the bus, and so did Fred.

Notice that the verb in the tag phrase of the combined sentence ("... Fred *did*, too.") matches the verb form used in the two sentences. Here's another example:

I like to play tennis. Ronald likes to play tennis.

a. I like to play tennis, and Ronald does, too.

b. I like to play tennis, and so does Ronald.

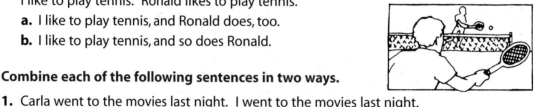

Combine each of the following sentences in two ways.

1. Carla went to the movies last night. I went to the movies last night.

a. _____

b. _____

2. Maddox can drive a car. Tom can drive a car.

a. _____

b. _____

3. Eduardo will graduate in June. I will graduate in June.

a. _____

b. _____

4. I could name all the presidents. Susana could name all the presidents.

a. _____

b. _____

5. My father is watching TV now. My sisters are watching TV now.

a. _____

b. _____

6. You have a bad cold. I have a bad cold.

a. _____

b. _____

7. Christina Aguilera is a singer. Madonna is a singer.

a. _____

b. _____

8. Fish live in the ocean. Whales live in the ocean.

a. _____

b. _____

SKILL OBJECTIVES: Combining sentences using *too* and *so*; choosing correct tenses; writing alternate forms of a sentence.
Go over the examples with the class. Be sure students understand why *did* is used in the first example and *does* in the second. Do all items orally with the class, then assign as independent written work. *Extension Activity:* Discuss other ways in which the sentences could be combined (*Ronald and I ...*, *Both Ronald and I ...*), and have students write additional answers for each item.

34

Either, Neither

Either and *neither* can be used to combine two negative statements into one. Look at the example. Notice that there are two ways of combining the sentences. One uses *either* and the other uses *neither*.

Susan doesn't like to play tennis. I don't like to play tennis.

    a. Susan doesn't like to play tennis, and I don't either.

    b. Susan doesn't like to play tennis, and neither do I.

Now combine the pairs of sentences below. Do each pair both ways.

1. I don't have any money. George doesn't have any money.

    a. _____

    b. _____

2. Hamid didn't go to work yesterday. I didn't go to work yesterday.

    a. _____

    b. _____

3. David can't speak Russian. Rosita can't speak Russian.

    a. _____

    b. _____

4. Ji Young isn't from Lebanon. Min Hee isn't from Lebanon.

    a. _____

    b. _____

5. Pedro wasn't in class yesterday. Carla and Anita weren't in class yesterday.

    a. _____

    b. _____

6. I won't graduate until next year. Linda and Nacho won't graduate until next year.

    a. _____

    b. _____

7. Kenneth isn't feeling well today. I am not feeling well today.

    a. _____

    b. _____

8. Mr. and Mrs. Garcia aren't going to buy a new car. You are not going to buy a new car.

    a. _____

    b. _____

9. Ahmed doesn't like Chinese food. I don't like Chinese food.

    a. _____

    b. _____

SKILL OBJECTIVES: Combining seintences with *either* and *neither*; writing alternate forms of a sentence. Review the use of *so* and *too* to combine positive sentences (page 34). Point out that negative sentences are combined another way, using *either* or *neither*. (Tell students that these can be pronounced with either a long *i* or long *e* sound; the long *e* is more common in the United States.) Go over the examples, then do all items orally before assigning as independent written work.

35

In the Newspaper: the Feature Article

Language Objectives
Answer questions about a reading. Write a news story.

Newspapers publish feature articles. A feature is not usually about something that has just taken place. Some features are humorous, designed to entertain the reader. Others provide information about subjects in which readers are likely to be interested. Newspaper editors may use different kinds of features on different days. They will have articles about books and the arts one day each week, and articles about business developments or about education another day, and science on still another day.

Read the article below and decide the category it belongs in.

ROTTEN WATER?

To most people, a lake they can look down into and see the bottom—or see fish swimming by—would be called clean. A sparkling lake that people can see through would also be called crystal or clear. That's the kind of lake you might think of swimming in. You might even think of opening your eyes underwater and looking around.

A scientist who studies water conditions would call a clear lake "oligotrophic." The scientific name means "few nutrients." The water in a clear oligotrophic lake is not full of algae. Algae are plants so small that you would need a microscope to see one of them. You don't need a microscope to see millions of them in a lake. When a lake has lots of algae, it is not clear. It is dull-looking. It is greenish, and there is scum in and on top of the water. It looks bad and smells bad. You would not want to swim in it. Opening your eyes under this water would be asking for trouble.

So, an oligotrophic lake may have some algae, along with some nutrients for other plants and fish. But an oligotrophic lake has a "few nutrients," or just the right amount. The sunlight can shine far down to the deepest parts of an oligotrophic lake.

The kind of lake that has too many algae in it, the scummy greenish lake, has a scientific name too. It is called a "eutrophic" lake. That means "many nutrients." A eutrophic lake has algae that not only live in it but have decayed over many years and have fallen to the bottom. As they decay, they use up the water's oxygen. You know that when something burns in the air, it oxidizes; it uses oxygen. In the water, when something rots, it uses up oxygen too. And sunlight cannot go down very far into this kind of water. A eutrophic lake is dark.

Left alone, clear oligotrophic lakes stay clear a long time, perhaps thousands of years. Eventually they may become eutrophic. However, people are dumping harmful things into rivers that flow into clear lakes. Such things as fertilizers and detergents are put into the lakes themselves. After a relatively short time, even the clearest oligotrophic lakes become clouded and thick-looking. The result of careless treatment is too many eutrophic lakes too soon.

There is hope. People can stop being careless. Communities, cities, states, and the federal government are beginning to pass laws to help keep rivers and lakes clean and sparkling. We all need to treat water with great care.

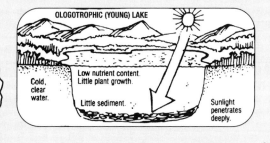

OLOGOTROPHIC (YOUNG) LAKE
Cold, clear water.
Low nutrient content. Little plant growth.
Little sediment.
Sunlight penetrates deeply.

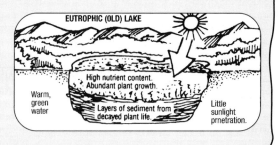

EUTROPHIC (OLD) LAKE
Warm, green water.
High nutrient content. Abundant plant growth.
Layers of sediment from decayed plant life.
Little sunlight prnetration.

(Go on to the next page.)

SKILL OBJECTIVES: Reading for details; understanding different types of informative writing; learning scientific/technical vocabulary; understanding scientific illustrations. Read the paragraph at the top of the page and discuss the difference between feature stories and news stories. Have students volunteer examples that point out the difference. Ask why many newspapers print a weekly science section; elicit the importance of science and technology in today's world. Preview some of the scientific vocabulary in the article and call attention to the way in which it is explained to the reader. Help students see how the illustrations reinforce ideas in the story. Allow time for students to read the story.

A   **Now answer these questions. Use complete sentences.**

1. What is an oligotrophic lake? _____

_____

_____

2. What is a eutrophic lake? _____

_____

_____

3. How do oligotrophic lakes become eutrophic lakes? _____

_____

_____

4. What kind of very small plant life is in a eutrophic lake? _____

_____

5. What is happening to plant life when a lake is greenish and smelly? _____

_____

_____

6. How long does it normally take a lake to change from oligotrophic to eutrophic?

_____

7. What happens when other people's activities add too many fertilizers and other nutrients

to a lake? _____

_____

B   *Olig-* and *eu-* are prefixes used in a number of words. Look up the following words in a dictionary and write a sentence using each one. Try to write your sentence so that the reader will understand the meaning of the word from context.

1. oligarchy   _____

2. oligopoly   _____

3. euphonious   _____

4. eupeptic   _____

C   **Find out about an environmental problem in your community. In your notebook, write a feature article that explains the problem, the effects of the problem, and possible solutions to the problem.**

SKILL OBJECTIVES: Reading for specific information; understanding cause and effect; writing a scientific/technical feature article. Discuss the article on page 36. *Part A:* Work through the seven questions orally as a class before assigning them as independent written work. *Part B:* Have students read their sentences aloud and explain them to the class. *Part C:* Talk about environmental issues in your area. Have students individually or in small groups pick an environmental issue that interests them and write a feature article about it. Refer them to local newspapers and magazines for specific information; your school librarian may be able to help. An encyclopedia or the Internet can be used to check technical facts.

Preparing for Tests: Stated and Implied Ideas (1)

Read the article.

The Petrified Forest

The Petrified Forest is not a real forest. At least it has not been one for many millions of years. The Petrified Forest National Park, located in Arizona, consists of 146 square miles of dry, sandy terrain. Within that area are several groups of fossilized trees, once an overgrown tropical forest. These fossilized logs, many of which lie on their sides rather than standing upright as in a living forest, come in many different colors.

The Painted Desert is located inside this park. In this area, wind has gradually made the landscape hilly through erosion. Over time, clay that was once underground has been exposed. The clays are bright yellow, red, or other colors, making the Painted Desert one of the more striking and beautiful parts of the United States.

Although its name might suggest that there is no life in it, the Petrified Forest is full of animals and plants. You might find anything from hummingbirds to lizards to snakes to bobcats prowling its rocks. And the variety of desert plants growing there ranges from sunflowers to evening primroses to cacti to yuccas.

Circle the best answer for each question.

1. The Painted Desert is
   a. in Arizona.   **b.** in Texas.   **c.** north of Pennsylvania.   **d.** in Scotland.

2. The Painted Desert contains all of the following except
   a. fossilized trees.   **b.** a lake.   **c.** lizards.   **d.** cacti.

3. What makes the Painted Desert colorful?
   a. The colors of the leaves on its trees.
   b. The color of the sunsets there.
   c. The beautiful minerals that can be found there.
   d. The clay exposed through erosion.

4. What does the first paragraph make you think *petrified* means?
   a. melting   **b.** cold   **c.** scared   **d.** turned to stone

5. You can assume that the author
   a. finds the Petrified Forest boring.
   b. was born in Arizona.
   c. finds the Petrified Forest interesting.
   d. goes hiking a lot.

SKILL OBJECTIVES: Reading for inference; finding specific information; understanding stated and implied ideas. This page, like page 28, is in a format typical of reading exercises in standardized tests. Reemphasize the importance of reading carefully but quickly. You may want to time the students so that they get used to pacing themselves on a reading passage and the associated questions. Six minutes is suggested as a time limit. After students have circled their answers, reread the passage orally, and have them give their answers to the questions. Discuss/explain all the answers, paying special attention to the inference questions and to tricky "distracters" (as in item 5, answer *b*).

Dear Dot

Dear Dot,

I am sixteen years old but very mature for my age. I am dating a twenty-three-year-old man. We enjoy each other's company but my parents are very much against our relationship. They say that Darrel is too old for me and that I should date boys my own age. I find boys my age boring and immature. I enjoy my relationship with Darrel and I don't want to give him up. How can I get my parents to leave me alone?

Sophisticated Lady

Discuss each of the questions in class. Then write your answers.

1. What do the words *mature* and *immature* mean in this letter?

_____

2. Do you think it is okay for a sixteen-year-old to date a twenty-three-year-old? Why or

why not? _____

_____

3. Should parents have the right to approve or disapprove of their teenage children's dates?

Why or why not? _____

_____

4. How can Sophisticated Lady work out a compromise with her parents? _____

_____

Write About It
Now put yourself in Dot's place. Write a helpful answer to Sophisticated Lady. Remember, you want to help solve her problem, not make fun of her or criticize her.

Dear Sophisticated Lady, _____

_____

_____

_____

_____

_____

SKILL OBJECTIVES: Reading for main idea; understanding words through context; making judgments; expressing opinions in writing. Have students read the letter. Discuss each question in class. Encourage free expression of opinion, but be sure opinions are supported, especially on the second and third questions. Then have students write answers, and use these as a basis for their letters. You may wish to assign the letter-writing activity as homework.

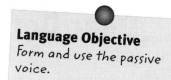

Language Objective
Form and use the passive voice.

Sentences in the active voice put the emphasis on the doer.

> Example: José ate the beans.

The emphasis is on José. Sentences in the passive voice change the emphasis.

> Example: The beans were eaten by José.

The emphasis is on the beans, rather than on José. The passive voice is formed using the appropriate form of the verb *to be* and the past participle of the main verb. In the example above, the active voice verb was in the past tense (*ate*), so the verb *to be* is in the past tense (*were*) when the sentence is changed to the passive. The passive voice is formed the same way in the present, past, future, and present perfect tenses. In each case, the tense of the verb *to be* in the passive sentence matches the tense of the main verb in the active sentence. Look at the examples below.

Active	Passive
William Shakespeare wrote *Hamlet*.	*Hamlet* was written by William Shakespeare.
People in Lebanon eat tabouli.	Tabouli is eaten by Lebanese people.
The police have arrested Tom.	Tom has been arrested by the police.

A Complete each of the passive sentences with one of the words from the Data Bank. The first one is done for you.

1. Portuguese is _____spoken_____ in Brazil.

2. Many stars are _____ only by astronomers.

3. Tiger Woods was _____ at Stanford University in California.

4. The Statue of Liberty was _____ to the United States by France.

5. The book *War and Peace* was _____ by Leo Tolstoy.

6. *Mona Lisa* and *The Last Supper* were _____ by Leonardo da Vinci.

7. The electric light bulb was _____ by Thomas Edison.

8. The mail was _____ very late yesterday.

DATA BANK

| written | delivered | educated | given | invented | painted | seen | ~~spoken~~ |

B Complete each of the following sentences by using the correct form of the verb *to be* and the past participle of the verb in parentheses. The first one is done for you.

1. Coffee (grow) _____is_____ _____grown_____ in Brazil.

2. My shoes (make) _____ _____ in Italy.

3. This book (publish) _____ _____ by Pearson Education.

4. The dinner (cook) _____ _____ too long, and it burned.

5. The sum of $500,000 (steal) _____ _____ from the bank.

6. The accident (see) _____ _____ by many witnesses.

7. Tools (sell) _____ _____ at hardware stores.

8. My shirt (make) _____ _____ of cotton.

SKILL OBJECTIVES: Forming and using the passive voice; distinguishing between active and passive. Read the introductory paragraph with the class, emphasizing the use and formation of the passive. Do the examples and ask volunteers for others. *Part A:* Do items 1 and 2 orally, then assign as independent written work. *Part B:* Call attention to the verbs in parentheses. Do items 1, 2, and 3 orally, then assign as written work. When students have finished, go over answers with the class to check understanding.

Who, What, When

Language Objectives

Practice the passive voice by matching historical events with the agents of those events. Turn sentences in the passive voice into active voice sentences.

A Match the two columns by writing the letter of the correct name or names next to the item in the first column that it goes with. Use the Internet or an encyclopedia if you need to. The first one is done for you.

1. The pyramids were built 4,000 years ago ___g___
2. Gaul was conquered in 51 BCE _____
3. Rome was conquered in 455 _____
4. England was invaded in 1066 _____
5. The Crusades were started in 1147 _____
6. The Magna Carta was signed in 1215 _____
7. Europe was devastated in 1348 _____
8. *Mona Lisa* was painted in 1400 _____
9. The movable type printing press was invented in 1454 _____
10. The New World was discovered in 1492 _____
11. The Sistine Chapel was painted in 1512 _____
12. The mercury thermometer was invented in 1714 _____
13. *Romeo and Juliet* was written in 1596 _____
14. The Declaration of Independence was written in 1776 _____
15. The Ninth Symphony was composed in 1824 _____
16. Abraham Lincoln was assassinated in 1865 _____
17. The phonograph was invented in 1877 _____
18. The first airplane was flown in 1903 _____
19. The world of physics was revolutionized in 1915 _____
20. Penicillin was discovered in 1928 _____
21. *Gone with the Wind* was written in 1936 _____
22. The helicopter was invented in 1939 _____
23. The Polaroid camera was invented in 1948 _____

a. by the Wright brothers.
b. by Ludwig van Beethoven.
c. by Albert Einstein.
d. by Michelangelo.
e. by Thomas Edison.
f. by John Wilkes Booth.
g. by the Egyptians.
h. by Thomas Jefferson.
i. by Dr. Alexander Fleming.
j. by Gabriel Fahrenheit.
k. by Julius Caesar.
l. by King John.
m. by William Shakespeare.
n. by Edwin Land.
o. by Pope Urban II.
p. by Johann Gutenberg.
q. by Igor Sikorsky.
r. by Leonardo da Vinci.
s. by Christopher Columbus.
t. by Margaret Mitchell.
u. by the bubonic plague.
v. by William the Conqueror.
w. by the Vandals.

B Check your work with your teacher. Then rewrite each sentence in your notebook using the active voice.

For example: The Egyptians built the pyramids 4,000 years ago.

SKILL OBJECTIVES: Understanding the passive voice; using reference books; placing historical events in time. *Part A:* Do the first three items with the group; discuss how they can find answers if they do not know them (review the use of the encyclopedia). Assign as independent work. Check answers in class when students have finished. *Part B:* Do the first three sentences orally, then assign as written work. *Extension Activity:* Have each student choose one of the items and write an essay about it.

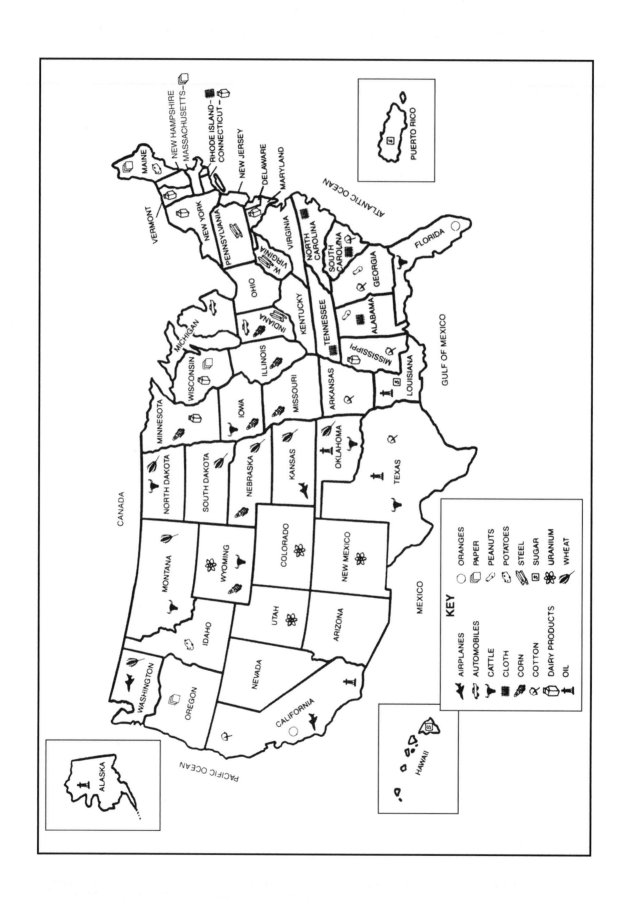

Where Is It Made or Grown?

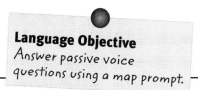

Language Objective
Answer passive voice questions using a map prompt.

The map on the opposite page shows some of the products of some of the states in the United States. Use the map and its "key" to answer the following questions. Use complete sentences. The first one is done for you.

1. In what two states are automobiles made?   *Automobiles are made in*
   Michigan and Indiana.

2. In what states are oranges grown? _____
   _____

3. Where is corn grown? _____
   _____

4. Where are airplanes made? _____
   _____

5. Where is cloth woven? _____
   _____

6. Where is steel produced? _____
   _____

7. Where are potatoes grown? _____
   _____

8. Where is oil found? _____
   _____

9. Where are cattle raised? _____
   _____

10. Where is sugar produced? _____
    _____

11. Where are dairy products made? _____
    _____

12. Where is paper manufactured? _____
    _____

13. Where is cotton grown? _____
    _____

14. Where is uranium found? _____
    _____

15. Where is wheat grown? _____
    _____

16. Where are peanuts grown? _____
    _____

SKILL OBJECTIVES: Interpreting a map with product symbols; forming and using the passive voice. Discuss the map on page 42.
Call attention to the key, and elicit that the symbols on the map show where different products come from. Be sure students understand such terms as *cattle* and *dairy products*. Point out that the map shows the principal products of states and the principal states that produce them, not all products and all producers. Go over the first five items orally, then assign as independent written work.

Applying for a Passport

Language Objectives
Answer questions about a reading. Write an expository paragraph that supports a topic statement.

You need a passport to travel to other countries outside the United States. A passport is a government-issued piece of identification with your photograph, your social security number, and other information about you. To get a passport, you have to go through an application process. This process is the same, regardless of where you happen to live.

Read the article, then answer the questions.

If you are applying for a passport for the first time, you have to apply in person. No one can do this for you. You also have to apply in person if your passport is no longer valid and you got it over fifteen years ago, if you are over fourteen but under twenty-one, if you changed your name since the last time you got a passport, if you lost your passport, or if you got your last passport when you were under 16 and it has now expired. If none of these are true for you, you can renew your passport by mail.

When you apply for a passport in person, you have to bring several things with you. One is an application form. You may get this form from a Passport Center near you. You may also download it off the following Web site: http://travel.state.gov/passport.

You also have to bring a document that proves you are a U.S. citizen. There are several documents that would serve this purpose. One is a birth certificate. This is a piece of paper your parents receive when you are born. It is government-issued identification, just like a passport, but it has no picture. If you do not have a birth certificate, you can order one. The certificates come in many different sizes. Some are almost as big as a piece of typing paper, and some are small enough to carry in your wallet.

If you were not born in the United States, you will not have a United States birth certificate. Therefore, you will need to bring a Consular Report of Birth Abroad or a Certification of Birth. These documents, issued by the embassy of your country, certify that you were born outside the United States.

If you are under fourteen, you have to present your application, along with a Birth Certificate, a previous passport, or other documents proving the place and time of your birth. Your parents also have to prove their relationship to you with a birth certificate or other documentation, as well as providing their own identification. They will also have to give written consent by filling out the proper form.

You will also need proof of identity—a driver's license or a previous passport. If you don't have these documents, you can use a library card and a Social Security card together. Alone, these documents do not prove identity. Also, someone who can prove your identity needs to come with you when you apply. This person has to be a United States citizen, has to have a valid ID, has to have known you for at least two years, and has to fill out Form DSP-71 in front of the agent to whom you are giving your application materials.

You need to supply two photos, two inches high by two inches wide, taken within the last six months. These photos can be either in color or in black and white. They should show you facing the camera directly, against a plain white background.

You need to pay a fee when you apply for a passport, as well. This fee will vary, depending on how you are applying. And last, but not least, you need to give a Social Security number. This number is important for identification. If you don't supply it, you could be fined by the Internal Revenue Service, the organization that collects taxes each year.

Once you have applied for a passport, the passport will be mailed to you. It usually takes several weeks for the application materials to be processed.

(Go on to the next page.)

SKILL OBJECTIVES: Reading for main idea and details; applying personal experience to interpretation of reading materials. Read the introductory paragraph with the class. Emphasize that the rules for applying for a passport are the same all over the United States. Ask if any students have passports or are in the process of getting them. After students read the article, discuss this question with the class.

A What are the steps you go through to get a passport? Put the following statements in chronological order, 1, 2, 3, etc.

_____ Leave the Passport Center.

_____ Present proof of your identity.

_____ Have two passport pictures taken.

_____ Fill out a passport application.

_____ Have someone who knows you well apply with you.

_____ Go to the Passport Center.

_____ Receive your passport in the mail.

B Read each of these statements. Decide if it is true or false. If it is true, circle the *T*. If it is false, circle the *F*.

1.	You can only apply for a passport in person.	T	F
2.	You can download an application form from the Internet.	T	F
3.	A birth certificate does not prove United States citizenship.	T	F
4.	The person who goes to the Passport Center with you does not have to know you.	T	F
5.	If you are not a United States citizen, you will never get a passport.	T	F
6.	If you are under fourteen, your parents have to give consent for you to get a passport.	T	F
7.	A driver's license is not a proof of identity.	T	F
8.	You must bring two photos with you when you apply.	T	F
9.	Your passport photos may only be in color.	T	F
10.	Your Social Security card and a library card can prove your identity.	T	F
11.	You can apply for a passport without a Social Security number.	T	F
12.	Passports are never sent through the mail.	T	F
13.	Processing a passport application can take several weeks.	T	F
14.	If you are under twenty-one, you cannot apply for a passport.	T	F
15.	You have to pay a fee when you apply for a passport.	T	F
16.	You can get a Consular Report of Birth Abroad at the post office.	T	F

C In your notebook, write a paragraph about why getting a passport could be useful.

SKILL OBJECTIVES: Sequencing; reading for details; expressing opinions in writing. *Part A:* Read the instructions with the class, then ask which of the sentences should be number 1. (Have two passport pictures taken.) Assign the remainder of the exercise as independent written work. *Part B:* Tell students they are to decide whether each statement is true or false according to the article on page 44. They may refer to the article as often as they wish. Do the first three items orally, then assign as written work. *Part C:* Lead a discussion about the usefulness of getting a passport. Then assign the paragraph as independent written work.

45

In the Newspaper: Advertisements

Language Objective
Answer questions about newspaper advertisements.

Many people use soap every day, to wash their hands, faces, bodies, clothes, and homes. Soap is manufactured all over the world. Hand soap is often made in bars. It may also come in a bottle, as liquid soap. People used to use soap to wash clothes and dishes. Now many people use detergent. Detergent comes in large bottles as a liquid or in a box as powder.

A Look at the advertisements below for soaps and detergents. Then answer the questions in your notebook. Use complete sentences. The first question is answered for you.

1. How much does E-Z Soap cost?   *E-Z Soap costs $3.59.*

2. What does Lite Soap smell like?

3. How does Tuff Detergent make your clothes look?

4. How does Splash Soap leave your hands feeling?

5. How do your hands often feel when washing dishes, according to the E-Z Soap ad?

6. How much more soap do you get with Splash Soap?

7. How would you describe the ingredients in Splash Soap?

8. What kind of smell does Tuff Detergent give your clothes?

9. What part of E-Z Soap gives added freshness?

(Go on to the next page.)

SKILL OBJECTIVES: Interpreting advertisements; reading for details; building vocabulary. Ask students to talk about the different kinds of soap used at their homes. Do the students like a certain soap smell? Or do they like soaps and detergents without much scent? Tell students they will be studying some ads for soaps. Read (or have students read) the introductory paragraphs. *Part A:* Have students read the ads, then use them to answer the questions. Do some or all questions orally, then assign as independent written work.

B Look at these ads for cleaning machines. Some of the tools you use to clean your home, like brooms or mops, are easy to find. Some of them are not so easy to find. You may have to order them. Sometimes smaller companies place ads in the classified sections of newspapers. Before ordering a product by mail, you should always be sure that the product is exactly what you want. Read the ads carefully. Be aware of ads that promise results that seem too good to be true.

Answer the questions about the ads in your notebook. Use complete sentences.

1. Most of the products listed can only be ordered over the phone. Which one can be ordered by mail?

2. What are the fibers of the broom offered here made from?

3. How much does the air purifier cost? In what colors is it available?

4. How much does the lightest Mighty-Vac weigh?

5. You are sneezing a lot in your home, and you do not have a cold. What products would you be likely to buy?

6. You just did a carpentry project that left a lot of sawdust on your hardwood floor. Which products would you be wise to purchase?

7. You just moved into an apartment with a very old air conditioner. What product here would you probably need to buy?

8. What qualities make the Dee-Luxe Air Filter a good buy?

9. What does it mean to say that models of the Mighty-Vac "start at only 10 pounds"?

10. What number do you call to order a Bestman broom?

C Write a description of a recent cleaning day or cleaning project at your home. Tell as much as you can about the different parts of it. What products were used? What parts of the home were easiest to clean? What parts were the most difficult?

D Imagine that you are trying to sell one of the products listed above. Write an ad for the product. What would you tell about the product that would make people reading the ad want to buy it? You are limited to five lines with no more than forty letters and spaces in a line. Remember: Each ad has to contain a telephone number, an address, or both.

SKILL OBJECTIVES: Interpreting advertisements; reading for details; writing descriptions; writing advertisements. The ads on page 46 are for different cleaning products. Most people buy these products regularly. *Part A:* Discuss the uses of the cleaning products mentioned on this page. Have students read the ads. Go over the questions orally, then assign as independent written work. *Parts C and D:* Discuss both activities in class before students write. You may wish to assign these as homework.

Restating Information

You can often express an idea in either of two ways. You can use the active voice or you can use the passive voice. Look at these sentences:

Rosa directed the class play.   Binh will pay for our lunch.

The class play was directed by Rosa.   Our lunch will be paid for by Binh.

Both sentences convey the same information. It is important to be able to express and understand ideas in both ways.

Look at the sentences below. Choose the sentence in the active voice that best expresses the idea of the sentence in the passive voice. Make sure that the tense remains the same in active and passive voice sentences.

1. The fish were caught by the boys at the river.
   a. The boys are catching fish at the river.
   b. The boys caught the fish at the river.
   c. The river was catching fish for the boys.

2. The tests are given by the professors every Saturday.
   a. The professors gave the test every Saturday.
   b. Every Saturday the tests give the professors.
   c. Every Saturday the professors give the tests.

3. You will be greeted at the airport by a man in a blue suit.
   a. You will greet a man in a blue suit at the airport.
   b. A man in a blue suit was greeted at the airport by you.
   c. A man in a blue suit will greet you at the airport.

4. Julie was given those earrings by her grandmother.
   a. Julie's grandmother gave her those earrings.
   b. Julie's grandmother was given those earrings by her.
   c. Julie's grandmother gives her those earrings.

5. Independence Day is celebrated on July 4th by Americans.
   a. Americans celebrated Independence Day on July 4th.
   b. Americans celebrate Independence Day on July 4th.
   c. July 4th celebrates Americans on Independence Day.

6. The winner was chosen at random by the judges.
   a. The winner chose the judges at random.
   b. The judges chose the winner at random.
   c. The judges will choose a winner at random.

7. I don't have my homework because it was eaten by my dog.
   a. The teacher didn't give homework so my dog didn't eat it.
   b. I don't feed my dog my homework but I don't have it.
   c. My dog ate my homework so I can't pass it in.

8. The winner's national anthem is played when the Olympic medal is awarded.
   a. The winner plays the national anthem for the Olympic award.
   b. They play the winner's national anthem when they award the Olympic medal.
   c. The Olympic medal plays the winner's national anthem as an award.

SKILL OBJECTIVES: Simplifying and restating information; understanding active and passive voice. Review the meaning of active and passive voice. Explain that the passive voice has tenses just as the active voice does (many students think all passives are past tense). Read the explanation in the box at the top of the page and make sure that all students understand that the two sentences in each pair convey the same meaning. Do item 1 as a class, then assign the page for independent work. Review all answers in class. After students have completed the exercise, have them generate their own sentences and change active ones to passive and passive ones to active.

48

Dear Dot

Dear Dot,

My oldest sister was killed in a car accident when she was nineteen years old. Now my parents say I can't get my license until my 21st birthday. My parents think that they are protecting me, but actually, they are doing the opposite. I am forced to ride with kids who are less responsible than I am. I am being deprived of driving experience, and also dating experiences. Many girls refuse to date a guy unless he has a car. How can I make my parents change their minds? When I bring up the subject, my father yells at me and my mother cries.

Carless in Arlington

Discuss each of the questions in class. Then write your answers.

1. Is Carless's parents' decision an emotional one or a logical one? How do you know?

What is the difference between these kinds of decisions? _____

_____

2. Does Carless make a good argument for having his license? Why or why not?

_____

3. Do you think his parents will be able to understand his need? Why or why not?

_____

4. Do you think peace in a family is more important than one individual's needs?

Explain your answer. _____

_____

Write About It

Now put yourself in Dot's place. Write a helpful answer to Carless. Remember, you want to help him solve his problem, not make fun of him or criticize him.

Dear Carless, _____

_____

_____

_____

_____

_____

_____

SKILL OBJECTIVES: Reading for main idea; reasoning deductively; making judgments; expressing opinions in writing. Have students read the letter. Discuss each question in class, with special attention to the first and fourth. Encourage free expression of opinion, but be sure opinions are supported. Then have students write answers to the questions (they may need extra paper). Suggest they use these answers as the basis for their letters. You may wish to assign the letter-writing activity as homework.

How much do you know about things that are American? Try this quiz. Circle your answers. After you have completed this quiz, discuss the answers in class. The first item is done for you.

1. Broadway is famous as the home of _____.
   a. concerts   **b.** hotels   (**c.** plays)   **d.** sports

2. The state famous for oil wells and cowboy boots is _____.
   a. Ohio   **b.** New York   **c.** Texas   **d.** California

3. Standing under the mistletoe can get you a _____.
   a. kiss   **b.** flower   **c.** cake   **d.** slap

4. Mark Twain is a famous American _____.
   a. singer   **b.** dancer   **c.** showman   **d.** author

5. The Exxon company is a large producer of _____.
   a. meat   **b.** sugar   **c.** coffee   **d.** gasoline

6. Abraham Lincoln is on the _____ bill.
   a. $5   **b.** $10   **c.** $1   **d.** $100

7. You go to the World Series to see _____.
   a. hockey   **b.** basketball   **c.** baseball   **d.** football

8. The car which is not American of the following is _____.
   a. Ford   **b.** Chevrolet   **c.** Pontiac   **d.** Jaguar

9. An Apple Mac is a _____.
   a. tree   **b.** computer   **c.** food   **d.** camera

10. You would most likely see the letters "Rx" in front of _____.
    a. schools   **b.** government buildings   **c.** drugstores   **d.** key shops

11. A Twinkie is a kind of _____.
    a. fish   **b.** star   **c.** cake   **d.** candy

12. One-A-Day is a famous _____.
    a. calendar   **b.** TV show   **c.** book   **d.** vitamin

13. Presley, Parton, and Wonder are famous _____.
    a. singers   **b.** lawyers   **c.** cars   **d.** shoes

14. The Hershey Company is famous for its _____.
    a. chocolate   **b.** donuts   **c.** sugar   **d.** hams

15. BLT is a name for a _____.
    a. margarine   **b.** pie maker   **c.** TV network   **d.** sandwich

16. Campbell's is famous for _____.
    a. tents   **b.** candy   **c.** soup   **d.** appliances

17. The country is split into East and West by the _____.
    a. White Mountains   **b.** Mississippi   **c.** border   **d.** Red River

18. Maxwell House is a famous kind of _____.
    a. coffee   **b.** hotel   **c.** restaurant   **d.** cake

19. The favorite food eaten at baseball games is _____.
    a. hamburgers   **b.** steak   **c.** hot dogs   **d.** pizza

20. The national bird of the United States is _____.
    a. the robin   **b.** the eagle   **c.** the turkey   **d.** the bluebird

SKILL OBJECTIVES: Building vocabulary; understanding American culture; taking multiple-choice tests. Tell the class that this page asks about many kinds of "things that are American." Point out that most students probably will not know the answers to many items, but that this is a chance to find out, since you will be discussing all the items after students have done the quiz. Stress that they should read all four choices before marking an answer; tell them to guess if they are not sure.

Analogies

An analogy is a comparison between two sets of words. Look at the example below. Which word completes the second set of words in a way that matches the first set of words?

hot : cold : : wet : _____   (You say: "Hot is to cold as wet is to _____")
water   dry   swim   warm

Clue: Put the first two words into a sentence that shows how those words fit together. "The opposite of *hot* is *cold*." Then substitute the second set of words into the same sentence: "The opposite of *wet* is _____."

Now complete each of the following analogies. Circle your answers.

1. nickel : five : : dime : _____
money   ten   dollar   one

2. puppy : dog : : colt : _____
kitten   horse   calf   tiger

3. green : grass : : white : _____
snow   winter   tree   black

4. twelve : dozen : : two : _____
doesn't   eggs   pair   eyes

5. hot : melt : : cold : _____
break   winter   heat   freeze

6. Thanksgiving : Thursday : : Easter : _____
spring   Sunday   vacation   April

7. write : written : : swim : _____
wrote   swam   swum   swimming

8. four : even : : seven : _____
nine   eleven   odd   number

9. thief : robber : : murderer : _____
killer   crime   steal   gun

10. author : book : : painter : _____
museum   artist   brushes   picture

11. mouse : mice : : tooth : _____
mouth   teeth   bite   tithe

12. question : answer : : ask : _____
reply   sentence   want   period

13. "post" : after : : "pre" : _____
soon   preview   before   again

14. watch : wrist : : ring : _____
look   finger   hand   bell

15. soldier : army : : player : _____
war   team   game   score

16. states : country : : teams : _____
league   sports   athletes   Olympics

17. play : acts : : book : _____
pretends   fiction   words   chapters

SKILL OBJECTIVES: Classifying words; reasoning logically; discovering relationships; building vocabulary. Discuss the concept of an analogy. Emphasize that the first two words may be related in any one of a number of different ways, and that the second two words must have the same relationship to each other as the first two. Go over the example and the clue; be sure students understand the idea. Do the first four items orally; have students name the relationship each time. Then assign as independent written work. *Extension Activity:* Have students write five analogies of their own.

What Will Happen . . . ?

Language Objective
State a future action based on a possible condition.

When you talk about something that may happen in the future, use the present tense in the first part of the sentence, and *will* or *may* in the second part.

> *If* the boy *steps* on the banana peel, he *will* slip.
>
> *If* the girl *falls* off her bike, she *may* get hurt.

Study the picture, then complete the sentences below.

1. If the man falls from the ladder, _____.

2. If the dog escapes from its leash, _____.

3. If the woman walks under the ladder, _____.

4. If the boy runs after the ball, _____.

5. If the boy doesn't run after the ball, _____.

6. If the car drives through the puddle, _____.

7. If the black cat walks in front of the man, _____.

8. If the bus stops, _____.

9. If the bus doesn't stop, _____.

10. If it rains, _____.

SKILL OBJECTIVES: Understanding cause and effect; using conditionals; expressing future action with *will* and *may*. Have students study the picture; review the various pictured situations orally and identify the actions. Read (or have a student read) the introductory paragraph; discuss the difference in meaning between *will* and *may*. Be sure students understand the sequence of tenses, then assign the questions as independent written work.

52

If You Forget

Language Objective
Predict a future action based on a possible condition.

A **Answer the following questions.**

1. If you forget to put ice cream in the freezer, what will happen?

   _____

2. If you drive too fast, what may happen?

   _____

3. If you mix red and yellow paint, what color will you have?

   _____

4. If it is raining and the temperature drops below 32°, what will happen?

   _____

5. If you forget to take back your library book when it is due, what will happen?

   _____

6. If you forget to pay the electric bill for two months, what may happen?

   _____

B **Finish the sentences below. The first one is done for you.**

1. If I leave my car windows open, _the seats may get wet._ _____

2. If they don't study for the test, _____

3. If you eat too much candy, _____

4. If Mary doesn't stop smoking, _____

5. If you don't come to class on time, _____

6. I'll bring my umbrella to school tomorrow if _____

7. I'll lend you my car if _____

8. Alfredo will have bad luck if _____

9. You will lose weight if _____

10. Carla won't pass the test if _____

SKILL OBJECTIVES: Understanding cause and effect; predicting outcomes; completing conditional sentences. *Part A:* Make sure students understand that the modals in the question should be repeated in the answer. Do all or some of the questions orally; try to get as many different answers to each question as possible. Assign as independent written work. *Part B:* Discuss why *may* is better than *will* in the first answer, then have students do the first five. Do questions 6 and 7 orally, eliciting different answers, then assign.

Could You Please Tell Me . . . ?

Language Objective
Learn and use question forms that indicate a formal level of discourse.

Questions often start with phrases such as the following:

Do you know . . . ?　　　　Could you please tell me . . . ?

Can you tell me . . . ?　　　Do you have any idea . . . ?

Example:　Where *is* Payton University?

　　　　　Can you tell me where Payton University *is*?

Example:　When *did* the movie *start*?

　　　　　Could you please tell me when the movie *started*?

Look at each question below. Change it to start with the polite phrase on the line. Notice that when you do this, the order of the words in the question is changed. Use the examples above as models for your answers.

1. How old is the President of the United States?

Do you know _____

2. How much does a pack of gum cost?

Can you tell me _____

3. When will the next bus arrive?

Could you please tell me _____

4. Where did my mother go?

Do you know _____

5. Where are my keys?

Do you have any idea _____

6. How did that package get here?

Can you tell me _____

7. What was our homework assignment?

Could you please tell me _____

8. Where will the test be given?

Can you tell me _____

9. How long has that woman been waiting?

Do you have any idea _____

10. How has the weather been in Florida?

Do you know _____

SKILL OBJECTIVES: Writing questions with polite introductory phrases; using correct word order. Lead a general discussion about manners and politeness. Why are they important? What purpose do they serve? Explain that certain phrases are used in English to show politeness, and read the examples at the top of the page. Elicit that the word order of the question is changed when the polite phrase is used. Then assign the page as independent written work.

54

Trivia Time

Work in groups of three or four to agree on answers to these questions. The group that can answer the most questions correctly wins.

A Write short answers.

1. When did Americans first land on the moon? _____

2. Who is the principal/director/head of this school? _____

3. How old must you be to vote in the United States? _____

4. In what state(s) are cars made in the United States? _____

5. What is a computer "bug"? _____

6. About how many people are there in this city/town? _____

7. What holiday do Americans celebrate in July? _____

8. When was the last big earthquake in California? _____

9. What does the term "cool" mean? _____

10. How many 37¢ stamps are there in a dozen? _____

11. How many months have 28 days in them? _____

12. Who created Mickey Mouse and Donald Duck? _____

13. What did Thomas Edison invent? _____

14. Where is the Golden Gate? _____

15. What was the *Mayflower*? _____

B Answer *yes* or *no*.

1. Is 16 the age people can get a driver's license in this state? _____

2. Could women vote in all states in the United States before 1920? _____

3. Have many Asians come to the United States in the past twenty years? _____

4. Is there a war anywhere in the world at this time? _____

5. Were Americans the first to travel in space? _____

6. Is coffee grown in the United States? _____

7. Did Columbus come to the Americas in 1942? _____

8. Is George W. Bush the President of the United States now? _____

9. Does February have only 28 days every year? _____

10. Was the Statue of Liberty given to the United States by France? _____

11. Does sound travel faster than light? _____

12. Is Boston farther north than Washington, D.C.? _____

13. Is Portuguese spoken in Brazil? _____

14. Is the Great Barrier Reef in Hawaii? _____

15. Did Peter Cooper invent the electric light? _____

SKILL OBJECTIVES: Reviewing/understanding cultural and historical information in a game situation. *Part A:* Divide the class into small groups, trying to balance abilities between and within groups. When students have finished (no time limit), go around each group and quietly record answers. Announce the winning group. Go over answers with the class. (You may want to create your own set of questions that are more appropriate to your class.) *Part B:* Do Part B as a class in another game situation, or assign it as written work. Again check the answers with the entire class. As an extension, you may wish to teach students how to answer if they don't know: "I don't know *when Americans first landed on the moon.*" "I don't know *if Americans were the first to travel in space.*"

In the Newspaper: the Editorial Page

Language Objectives
Answer questions about a reading. Write a newspaper editorial.

News articles try to present only *facts*. The editorial page is the section of the newspaper where news writers are given the opportunity to express their *opinions* about recent events, policies, trends, and community activities.

Read the editorial below, then answer the questions.

THE TELEVISION HABIT

It is time for responsible parents to pull the plug on television. Ninety percent of television programs shown today are a waste of time and an offense to any intelligent person, adult, or child. People must begin to say *no* to television, to refuse to let it interfere with their lives. They must find other hobbies and pastimes. Televisions across the country must be turned off.

It is estimated that most children watch three to five hours of television per day. Imagine the amount of constructive work that could be done in this time—the books that could be read, the chores that could be done—it staggers the mind. Yet, across the nation, parents continue to allow their children free access to television. Test scores are plunging and the rate of functional illiteracy is increasing, but nothing is done.

Turning off the television and forcing children to account for their free time is the first step in changing a wasteful national habit.

1. What is the writer's opinion of television? _____

_____

_____

2. What fact does the writer give about the TV viewing habits of American children?

_____

3. What does the phrase "functional illiteracy" mean? _____

_____

4. What does the author think is the reason that test scores have plunged and the level of high school literacy has become lower? _____

5. Is this an opinion or a fact? _____

6. Which phrase best describes the tone of the editorial (the author's attitude or feelings towards the subject)?

    a. light-hearted, humorous   **c.** calm and reasonable

    b. forceful and demanding   **d.** willing to compromise

(Go on to the next page.)

SKILL OBJECTIVES: Distinguishing between fact and opinion; making inferences, reading for detail; establishing tone. Read (or have a student read) the introductory paragraph and discuss what an editorial is. Then have students read the editorial silently. *Part A:* Assign the first five questions. Then discuss the idea of "tone," and read the editorial aloud in a "forceful and demanding" manner; assign the sixth question. *Extension Activity:* Have students read other editorials (they may bring them in) and establish their tone.

B The editorial page also contains letters to the editor. These letters are written by people in the community. The letters may comment on local or national events and trends, or they may respond to previous editorials or letters to the editor. Letters to the editor are written to express an opinion. The writer usually includes certain facts that support his or her viewpoint. Look at the statements below about television viewing in America. Some of the statements are facts and some are opinions.

Write *F* after each fact, and *O* after each opinion.

Statements About Television Viewing in America

1. TV has broadened people's experiences and enriched their lives. _____

2. Without TV, most Americans would never see the President speak or watch a major league ball game, or learn about wild animals by seeing them in their native environment. _____

3. In the average American home, at least one TV set is on for six hours every day. _____

4. Television shows present an unrealistic picture of American life. _____

5. Television keeps elderly people young at heart and interested in life by keeping them informed about world events and involving them in the problems and feelings of TV characters. _____

6. The average American child spends more time sitting and watching TV than in any other single waking activity. _____

7. Every television set is equipped with an ON/OFF button. _____

8. Violence is common on many TV shows, but particularly in cartoons geared to children. _____

9. Watching violent programs on TV causes people to act more violently. _____

10. Educational TV programs have successfully taught many children early reading and number skills in an entertaining way. _____

C Now write a letter to the editor responding to "The Television Habit." You may agree or disagree with the editorial. You may bring up other sides of the issue. You may want to tell what points of the editorial you particularly agree or disagree with. Your letter should contain both opinions and facts. Include only those facts that support your opinion.

Dear Editor,

_____

_____

_____

_____

_____

_____

_____

_____

SKILL OBJECTIVES: Distinguishing between fact and opinion; expressing and supporting an opinion in writing. *Part B:* Do the first three items orally, reviewing the difference between fact and opinion. Then assign as independent written work. *Part C:* Suggest that students use material from Part B for their letters if they wish to. Read the instructions and discuss the kinds of things students will include in their letters. Then assign, perhaps as homework. *Extension Activity:* Bring in and analyze letters to the editor.

57

Saying It Another Way

Language Objective
Restate or interpret questions using a less formal level of discourse.

It is important to be able to understand different ways of asking questions or expressing ideas. The exercise below will give you practice in restating questions.

Circle the sentence that is most similar in meaning to the numbered one.

1. Would you mind if I borrowed your notes?
   a. Lend me your notes, please.
   b. I borrowed your notes.
   c. I minded your notes.
   d. Can I lend you my notes?

2. Could you tell me where the theater is located?
   a. I don't want to know where the theater is.
   b. Where is the theater, please?
   c. Please give me directions to the library.
   d. When will you be going to the theater?

3. Do you know when the next plane will be departing?
   a. Has the next plane arrived yet?
   b. What time is the next plane scheduled to take off?
   c. When did the plane depart?
   d. I can't take off on the next plane because I'm not packed.

4. Do you have any idea what the weather will be like tonight?
   a. You can never be sure about the weather.
   b. Doesn't anyone like the weather we are having tonight?
   c. Do you like this weather?
   d. Do you know anything about tonight's weather forecast?

5. Would it be all right if I gave you some advice?
   a. Would you like my opinion?
   b. Would you give me some advice about my problems?
   c. Would it be all right if I took your advice?
   d. I should have listened to your advice.

6. You don't mind if I come along to the dance, do you?
   a. You don't want me to dance with you.
   b. Is it okay if I come to the dance with you?
   c. You're out of your mind if you expect me to dance.
   d. I hope you don't mind, but I can't go to the dance.

7. Could you explain why so many people are afraid of mice?
   a. I'm trying to explain why mice frighten me.
   b. I don't understand why mice frighten me.
   c. I don't understand why mice frighten so many people.
   d. Most people aren't afraid of mice, are they?

SKILL OBJECTIVES: Simplifying and restating information; understanding different levels of discourse; understanding various question forms. Explain that sometimes in formal situations, a more "polite" form of English is customary, especially in asking questions or seeking permission. In each item, the numbered question is in the polite, formal form. Students are to find the other sentence that says the same thing. You may wish to do one or two items orally as a class before assigning the page for independent written work.

Fact or Opinion?

**Facts are true statements that can be checked and proven.
Opinions are what a person thinks or feels about something.**

A **Read each sentence below and decide if it states a fact or an opinion. Write *F* after each fact and *O* after each opinion.**

1. April 15 is the deadline for some federal tax payments. _____

2. Water freezes at 32° Fahrenheit. _____

3. You can never be too rich or too thin. _____

4. Nothing is more important than your health. _____

5. Beethoven was the greatest musical composer who ever lived. _____

6. Many words in English have Latin roots. _____

7. The pyramids are early civilization's greatest accomplishment. _____

8. There are 206 bones in the human skeleton. _____

9. The Chinese alphabet has over 3,000 characters. _____

10. Early to bed, early to rise, makes a man healthy, wealthy, and wise. _____

11. Rock music is for teenagers only. _____

12. Odd numbers are numbers that can't be divided by 2. _____

13. Neil Armstrong walked on the moon in 1969. _____

14. Panda bears are native to China. _____

15. Everyone should have a college education. _____

16. You can't teach an old dog new tricks. _____

17. The sun is a small star compared to many others in the sky. _____

18. A prime number can only be divided by 1 and itself. _____

19. There is no life in outer space. _____

20. Plane travel is the most efficient means of transportation. _____

21. The medical profession is the most noble. _____

22. Pluto is the planet most distant from the sun. _____

23. It's important for young children to play musical instruments. _____

24. You can't judge a book by its cover. _____

25. Christopher Columbus was born in Genoa, Italy. _____

B **Find an opinion on this page that you agree with. Then in your notebook, write a paragraph of five or six sentences that supports the opinion. Start your paragraph with "I think ..." or "My opinion is ..." and tell why you agree with the opinion.**

SKILL OBJECTIVE: Distinguishing between fact and opinion. *Part A:* Make sure students understand that this is not a true/false exercise. Point out that all the statements are either factually true or true as the opinions of some person or persons; the student must decide which. Point out that some of the statements are proverbs, and make sure that students understand that even though a proverb can be thought of as a kind of "universal truth," it is an opinion and not a fact. *Part B:* Discuss the fact that most people have reasons for their opinions. Ask several volunteers to read an opinion on the page with which they agree and discuss why they agree with it. Then assign Part B for independent written work, perhaps as homework.

Dear Dot

Language Objectives
Answer questions about a reading. Give advice. Agree or disagree with advice.

Dear Dot,

My father is constantly criticizing me for the way I dress. He says that my dresses are too short and my jeans are too tight. And, of course, he thinks I use too much make-up. I have tried to explain to him about fashion but he just doesn't want to understand. He thinks I look "cheap." I tell him that's his opinion. My friends all dress the same way and their parents seem to accept it. What can I do?

Dress Code Blues

Discuss each of the questions in class. Then write your answers.

1. What does *criticize* mean? _____

_____

2. What is "constructive criticism?" _____

_____

3. Do you think the father is giving constructive criticism? Explain your answer.

_____

_____

4. Should a parent have the right to control what a teenager wears? Why or why not?

_____

_____

5. How can Dress Code Blues work out a compromise with her father? _____

_____

Write About It

Now put yourself in Dot's place. Write a helpful answer to Dress Code Blues. Remember, you want to help solve the problem, not make fun of her or criticize her.

Dear Dress Code Blues,

_____

_____

_____

_____

_____

_____

SKILL OBJECTIVES: Reading for details; building vocabulary; making judgments; expressing opinions in writing. Discuss the meanings of *criticize*, and elicit that its connotation is usually negative; help students contrast this with *constructive criticism*. Discuss each of the other questions, then have students write their answers. Suggest that they use these answers as a basis for their letters. You may wish to assign the letter-writing activity as homework.

He Used to Be Messy

Language Objective
Answer questions comparing past and present.

Read the story.

Michael's room used to be very messy. It used to be a real problem for him. Then one day he lost his favorite CD in his room. When he cleaned his room, it took him all day, but he found it. Now he cleans his room once a week. His music stuff used to be all over the place. Now it's all on a shelf.

Before, he had so much trouble. He used to lose his pencils. Now he keeps them in a cup on his desk. He used to trip on tennis shoes lying around. Now he keeps the shoes in his closet. He used to leave his papers on the floor. Now he keeps them in a file cabinet. He used to bring food in his room at night and leave it under a sock or a jersey. Phew! Now he eats only in the kitchen at night. His parents are amazed and very pleased. So is Michael. He can hardly believe himself.

Answer the questions below. Use complete sentences. The first one is done for you.

1. How did Michael's room use to look?   _His room used to be very messy._

2. What did he lose in his room?   _____

3. How did he find what he lost?   _____

4. What does his room look like now?   _____

5. Where did he use to put his music stuff?   _____

6. Where does he put his music stuff now?   _____

7. What used to happen to his pencils?   _____

8. What does he do with his pencils now?   _____

9. Where did he use to leave his papers?   _____

10. Where does he keep his papers now?   _____

11. What did he use to trip on?   _____

12. How does he keep from tripping now?   _____

13. Where did he use to leave food at night?   _____

14. Where does he eat at night now?   _____

SKILL OBJECTIVES: Expressing past action with *used to*; reading for specific information; comparing and contrasting. Have students look at the illustrations and discuss them. Then have the paragraph between the illustrations read silently. Call attention to the repeated phrase *used to* and explain it as indicating continued action in the past that does not continue to the present. Do the first six items orally. Then assign the page as independent written work.

What Should You Do?

A Read the chart below, then write sentences with *should, ought to,* or *had better*. The first two are done for you.

Problem	Solution
Salma has the hiccups.	Drink some water.
Lara is very tired.	Get more rest.
Marta and Leiko have stomachaches.	Lie down.
Mr. Rossi drives very fast.	Slow down.
My car is making funny noises.	Take it to a mechanic.
You have a sore throat.	Gargle with salt and water.

1. _Salma has the hiccups. She had better drink some water._

2. _Lara is very tired. She ought to get more rest._

3. _____

4. _____

5. _____

6. _____

B What do you think you should do in the following situations? Write your answers on the lines. Use complete sentences.

1. You see a strange man entering a neighbor's house through a window. What should you do? _____

    _____

2. It is a very cold day and there's no heat in your apartment. What should you do?

    _____

3. Your friend, Lola, smokes three packs of cigarettes a day. What should you do?

    _____

4. Your friend, George, has to take an important history test tomorrow morning. You are at a nightclub together now, and it's getting late. What should you do?

    _____

5. You and your friends are playing baseball in your backyard. You hit the ball through a neighbor's window. What should you do? Who should pay for the window? You? The team? Your neighbor? _____

    _____

SKILL OBJECTIVES: Using modals *should, ought to, had better*; making judgments; writing solutions to problems. *Part A:* Elicit that all three modals have approximately the same meaning (obligation or logical necessity). Make sure students understand when to use the completer *to.* Call attention to the chart and the two "done for you" sentences, then have students write sentences for the other problems. *Part B:* Do all items orally, eliciting several responses for each, then assign as independent written work.

62

It's Possible!

Language Objective
Express possible outcomes of situations using <u>may</u>, <u>might</u>, and <u>will</u>.

A Read the chart below, then fill in the missing possibilities. Your class will come up with many different answers.

Present Facts	Possibilities
Mohammad is sneezing.	**a.** He has an allergy. **b.** He has a cold.
Osato and Pedro never eat candy.	**a.** They are on a diet. **b.** They don't like candy.
Laura is not in class today.	**a.** **b.**
It's 9:00 p.m. and the lights are out next door.	**a.** **b.**

B Now write sentences about situations on the chart. Use *may* or *might* plus the simple form of the verb. The first two are done for you.

1. _Mohammad might have an allergy or he might have a cold._

2. _Osato and Pedro may be on a diet or they may not like candy._

3. _____

4. _____

C Read the chart, then fill in the missing possibilities.

Facts About the Future	Possibilities
Callie is going to graduate soon.	**a.** She will get a job. **b.** She will go to college.
Antonio is going to buy a new car.	**a.** He will buy a Ford. **b.** He will buy a Toyota.
Anna is going to college next year.	**a.** **b.**
I am going to take a vacation.	**a.** **b.**

D Write sentences about the situations on the chart. Use *may* or *might* and the simple form of the verb. The first one is done for you.

1. _Callie might get a job or she might go to college._

2. _____

3. _____

4. _____

SKILL OBJECTIVES: Expressing possibility with *might* or *may*; making inferences; drawing conclusions. *Part A:* Complete the chart orally, asking for as many responses as possible. *Part B:* Have students use the chart to write sentences, using the two completed items as models. Be sure students understand the changes in verb form between the chart and the response sentences. *Parts C and D:* Follow the same procedure as for Parts A and B. Point out that *might* and *may* can be used with statements about both present and future.

63

Harry Houdini

Read the article.

If you were a young person in the early 1900s, you probably would have been very familiar with the name Harry Houdini. Just the mention of his name would have excited you. You might have saved up all of your allowance to buy a ticket to one of his shows. You might have waited in line for hours to see him perform. Was he a famous singer? Was he a famous dancer? Did he play with a band? Did he play the violin or the piano? The answer to all of these questions is "No." But Harry Houdini *was* a great performer. Houdini was one of the greatest performers of all time. He dazzled audiences all over the world with his breathtaking escapes. How did Houdini become one of the most famous entertainers in the world?

Harry Houdini was born in 1874 in Budapest, Hungary. When he was four years old, his parents moved to Appleton, Wisconsin. His father was Rabbi Mayer Samuel Weiss. Harry Houdini's real name was Erich Weiss. Young Erich had to work to bring in money for the family, but he still found time to enjoy himself. He was very athletic and liked several different sports. One sport he enjoyed was swimming. Another activity the young boy enjoyed was doing magic tricks.

When he grew up, he lived in New York, where he and a friend started performing magic tricks in a magic act. They called themselves "The Brothers Houdini" after Jean-Eugene Robert-Houdin, the father of modern magic. They did less-than-amazing magic tricks, but people still came to watch.

When Houdini was twenty, he fell in love and married. His lifestyle—traveling from place to place and earning very little money—made things difficult for the young couple. But better things were coming.

A man named Martin Beck came to see one of the shows. Beck booked theater acts.

He was interested in Houdini's "magic" escapes from handcuffs. Beck offered Houdini a whole season of work. It was a wonderful opportunity. Better things had certainly come!

Soon Houdini was performing in theaters everywhere. He was now known as an escape artist. His performances became more and more exciting. Sometimes for attention, Houdini would perform stunts in public where great crowds would gather to watch.

Houdini's theater audiences were growing, too. His fame in the United States had spread from coast to coast. And his fame had spread to Europe, too. So he decided to tour Europe. After several years of being welcomed in the different countries of Europe, Houdini returned to America.

Houdini continued to work hard perfecting his escapes and taking on new challenges. He came up with the idea for the Milk Can Escape, which became one of his most famous escapes. In this escape, he tempted fate. A huge milk can was filled with water. If Houdini did not escape in time, he would drown. The strong swimming skills he developed when he was young helped him now. Audiences went wild with excitement.

Surprisingly, another interest of Houdini's was aviation. He is credited with completing the first airplane flight, in Australia, in 1910.

Houdini went on to develop more and more escapes. He even jumped from bridges in handcuffs and chains. One escape was the Upside-Down Water Torture Escape. For this, Houdini's ankles were fastened and he was placed upside down in a water-filled chamber and locked in place. It was an escape that challenged his physical power and stunned audiences with its drama. This may have been Houdini's most amazing trick.

(Go on to the next page.)

SKILL OBJECTIVES: Reading for main idea and details; building vocabulary. Ask students if they have heard of Harry Houdini. Some may have seen a movie or TV program about him; allow discussion of what they know about him. Then preview the following vocabulary: *entertainers, lifestyle, opportunity, escape artist, stunts, fame, perfecting, aviation, challenges, fastened, chamber, vanish, spirit world, appendix, infection.*

In 1918, an audience watched as Houdini made a huge elephant "vanish" right before their eyes. People kept coming to see Houdini's performances in theaters, but by this time in America people were enjoying a new form of entertainment. They were going to the movies. The movies were silent, but everyone loved the movies. It was then that Harry Houdini decided to entertain audiences by performing in movies. His first film was called *The Master Mystery*. In that movie, he played one of the first action heroes. Audiences had mixed opinions about his acting ability.

Another subject that caught Houdini's attention in the early 1920s was the popularity of spiritualists. Spiritualists were people who claimed they could contact the spirit world and talk to the dead. People were giving spiritualists their hard-earned money with the hopes of talking to their lost loved ones. Houdini believed that these spiritualists were tricksters and wanted to warn people against them. Some people really believed in the spiritualists, so

Houdini's war against the spiritualists brought him both positive and negative attention.

In 1926, Houdini had a one-man show on Broadway in New York City. Later, he took that show to theaters in different cities. During a stay in Montreal, Canada, Houdini took on one more challenge, one that proved fatal. He allowed himself to be punched by a young man as a test of his strength. Houdini did not know it, but at the time he had appendicitis. Appendicitis is an inflammation of the appendix. Houdini was in great pain and had to have his appendix removed. But then he developed a deadly infection.

Harry Houdini died on Halloween night, October 31, 1926, in Detroit, Michigan. What a remarkable thing—to have this man, who was such a mystery to so many people, die on the most mysterious night of the year!

You may be interested in reading more about Harry Houdini, or books written by him. And someday you may even have the chance to visit the Houdini Historical Center in Appleton, Wisconsin.

A Read each statement below and decide if it is a fact or an opinion. Circle *F* if it is a fact. Circle *O* if it is an opinion.

1. Houdini was born in 1874 in Budapest, Hungary.   F   O

2. His early magic tricks were less than amazing.   F   O

3. Houdini probably thought his wife was beautiful.   F   O

4. Martin Beck was a kind man.   F   O

5. Houdini became one of the greatest performers of all time.   F   O

6. Houdini did a trick with a milk can.   F   O

7. Houdini traveled to Europe where he performed.   F   O

8. Houdini was a wonderful actor.   F   O

9. Spiritualists can talk to the dead.   F   O

10. It was foolish for Houdini to allow himself to be punched.   F   O

11. Houdini had an infection from appendicitis.   F   O

12. Houdini died on Halloween night.   F   O

13. The Houdini Historical Center is located in Appleton, Wisconsin.   F   O

14. You would enjoy a visit to the Houdini Historical Center.   F   O

B People say that "seeing is believing." What do you think makes people believe what they see with their own eyes? Can people "see" something, only later to find out that it is just not real? In your notebook, write a paragraph about what you think makes people "believe what they see," or "think they see." Share your paragraph with the class. You will see there are many different ideas about the saying "seeing is believing."

SKILL OBJECTIVES: Distinguishing between fact and opinion; expressing opinions in writing; interpreting proverbs. *Part A:* Review the differences between fact and opinion and true/false exercises, then assign the items. When students have finished, ask for other facts in the story and discuss the characters. *Part B:* Discuss the meaning of the saying "seeing is believing." Ask students to give examples of when they saw something unusual but believed it because they saw it with their own eyes. You may wish to assign the paragraph writing as homework.

I Would Rather Stay Home

Would rather means "to prefer." Read the example below.

Would you rather go to a movie or watch TV tonight?
I'd (I would) rather stay home and watch TV.

A **Answer the questions. Tell what you would rather do. The first one is done for you.**

1. Would you rather live in the country or in the city?

   I'd rather live in the city.

2. Would you rather learn French or Chinese?

   _____

3. Would you rather be a doctor or a lawyer?

   _____

4. Would you rather play the piano or the guitar?

   _____

5. Would you rather drive a Ford or a Toyota?

   _____

6. Would you rather be the oldest or the youngest in a family?

   _____

7. Would you rather wash the dishes or vacuum the living room?

   _____

8. Would you rather go to a big party or go out with a few friends?

   _____

B **What would these people rather do? Look at the picture, then answer the question. The first one is done for you.**

1. Susan ➔ wear jeans / a dress

   Susan would rather wear jeans than a dress.

2. Raul ➔ listen to CDs / clean his room

   _____

3. We ➔ drink coffee / orange juice

   _____

4. Maria and Pacha ➔ play tennis / soccer

   _____

5. My mother ➔ live in an apartment / a house

   _____

6. They ➔ stay in a hotel / go camping

   _____

SKILL OBJECTIVES: Expressing Reference with _would rather_. Elicit that the use of _would rather_ implies a stated or unstated alternate to the action with which it is used. Be sure students understand that _would rather_ does not take the completer _to_; such small details are important in written and oral communication, and errors are noticeable to native speakers. _Part A_: Read and discuss the instructions, then assign as independent written work. _Part B_: Tell students to use the illustrations as clues for their answers.

Take It With a Grain of Salt

Slang expressions don't mean what they seem to say. They have special meanings that must be learned. Try to match the slang expressions in Column A to their meanings in Column B. The dictionary explains many of these expressions. Use the dictionary if you need help. The first item is done for you.

A

1. Have you buried the hatchet? _____s_____

2. Kill two birds with one stone. _____

3. It's raining cats and dogs! _____

4. You let the cat out of the bag. _____

5. Did you foot the bill? _____

6. Did you learn it by heart? _____

7. You gave them the cold shoulder. _____

8. Did you get cold feet? _____

9. We don't see eye to eye. _____

10. We were shooting the breeze. _____

11. Hold your horses! _____

12. No use crying over spilt milk. _____

13. You have to face the music. _____

14. Are you down in the dumps? _____

15. Are you moonlighting? _____

16. Are you going Dutch? _____

17. You hit the nail on the head. _____

18. Have you tied the knot? _____

19. You passed with flying colors! _____

20. You didn't cut the mustard. _____

21. Don't knock it! _____

22. You pulled a fast one. _____

23. You swallowed it hook, line, and sinker. _____

24. You have bats in your belfry. _____

25. Let's hit the hay. _____

B

a. Did you get married?

b. Did you pay for everybody?

c. You must confront the problem.

d. Get both things done at the same time.

e. We don't agree.

f. Don't criticize or make fun of it.

g. Are you paying your own way? (on a date)

h. That's exactly right.

i. We were just talking.

j. You didn't do well enough.

k. You were unfriendly to them.

l. Do you have a second job?

m. It's raining very hard.

n. You tricked somebody.

o. Don't worry about something that's already been done.

p. You got a very good grade.

q. Did you memorize it?

r. Did you get scared and decide not to do it?

s. Have you made peace?

t. You're crazy!

u. You told the secret.

v. Wait a minute!

w. Let's go to bed.

x. Are you depressed?

y. You believed it completely.

SKILL OBJECTIVE: Interpreting figurative language. Read (or have a student read) the introductory paragraph and discuss it with the class; make sure students understand the concept of slang expressions; ask volunteers for some from their native languages. If practical, do the page as a group activity; this way the collective knowledge of the group is shared (and an opportunity is provided for free communication). If some phrases stump the class, discuss use of the process of elimination and "educated guessing."

67

In the Newspaper: Daily Features and Word Games

Most newspapers have daily features. One kind of daily feature you might see is an article about health. Read the following information from a health article. Then answer the questions in your notebook.

CHOOSE FOODS WISELY
By J. H. Darcy

Every day, readers of newspapers may read articles on diets and dieting. Advice is free for the taking. But, when you think about your diet, don't forget some important things. Here are things to think about when planning meals for your good health.

- You should drink plenty of water each day.
- You should eat three meals a day.
- You should limit eating foods with high amounts of refined sugars.
- You should limit eating foods with high amounts of saturated fats.
- You may want to include lean meats and fish for protein.
- You ought to eat low-fat dairy products, such as low-fat or skim milk.
- You should add foods rich in calcium, such as yogurt or broccoli, for strong bones.
- You may vary the fruits and vegetables you choose.
- You may want to eat whole wheat bread instead of white bread.
- You might think about snacking on vegetables instead of chips.
- You ought to ask your doctor if you should take a daily vitamin.
- You might want to check with your doctor before beginning an exercise program.

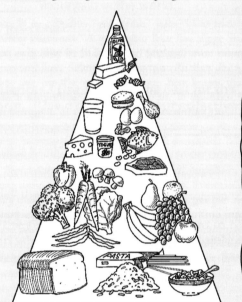

 A

1. Why may you want to include lean meats in your diet?
2. Why may you choose to eat broccoli?
3. Why may it be good to vary the fruits and vegetables you eat?
4. Which kinds of foods should you limit eating?
5. Which other kinds of foods should you limit eating?
6. What should you drink a lot of every day?
7. How many meals should you have each day?
8. Who should you ask about taking vitamins?
9. What snack might be better for your health than chips?
10. What is a low-fat dairy product?
11. What kind of bread might you try instead of white bread?
12. Who should you ask before starting an exercise program?

(Go on to the next page.)

SKILL OBJECTIVES: Reading for main ideas and details. Have students read the complete page, then reread it, underlining all of the words that show possibility or future time. *Extension Activity:* Discuss the value of having a daily feature about health. Point out that newspaper articles are general enough that many people can benefit from reading them. Students might bring in several different daily newspaper articles for the same day and compare them.

Many newspapers have word games and puzzles. The word game below is a word search. Look for letters that make a word and circle the word. First look across, and then down. Find fifteen words about a healthy diet.

```
I  W  O  R  G  E  G  A  R  A  P  P  L  E  T
Y  P  E  A  R  A  M  E  Z  A  T  S  A  G  L
D  E  T  S  A  L  E  T  T  U  C  E  G  G  A
O  L  U  B  R  M  A  D  P  G  I  E  E  L  M
R  E  F  R  U  I  T  S  E  P  W  P  L  C  S
A  M  F  E  C  L  C  R  U  N  A  A  E  A  A
N  O  E  A  E  K  V  E  G  E  T  A  B  L  E
G  C  D  D  I  F  I  S  H  E  E  S  C  C  T
E  E  I  C  G  I  H  C  S  R  R  D  I  I  H
I  C  A  R  R  O  T  E  T  A  M  T  E  U  Y
A  O  N  I  S  D  E  S  U  G  A  R  A  M  S
P  R  O  T  E  I  N  E  D  S  V  B  I  K  A
```

Write each word you found on a line below.

1. _____   6. _____   11. _____

2. _____   7. _____   12. _____

3. _____   8. _____   13. _____

4. _____   9. _____   14. _____

5. _____   10. _____   15. _____

Here's another kind of word game that may be found daily in some newspapers. There is a riddle next to the picture. To solve the puzzle, read the five sentences and fill in the missing words. Find the numbered letters and copy them into the spaces to complete the riddle.

Question: What happened in Alaska to the daring young man on the flying trapeze?

Answer:

He ____ ____ ____   ____ ____ ____ ____   ____ ____ ____ ____
    3   2   10   6   4   1   5   8   7   11   9

1. The ribbon was four inches _____.   ____ ____ ____ ____
                                             1   2

2. _____ is a metal used for jewelry.   ____ ____ ____ ____
                                              3   4   5

3. The boys ate six _____ of cake.   ____ ____ ____ ____ ____ ____
                                                        6   7

4. The opposite of thin is _____.   ____ ____ ____
                                          8   9

5. Some people _____ vitamins.   ____ ____ ____ ____
                                       10   11

SKILL OBJECTIVE: Solving a puzzle. *Part A:* Do the questions orally; ask for answers in complete sentence form and be sure students use the modals from the questions in their answers, then have them write short answers for the questions. *Part B:* Assign for independent work. *Part C:* Review the instructions and then have students work in pairs to complete the puzzle. (The answer is on page 117.)

Find the Error (1)

There is a grammatical error in one of the underlined words or phrases in each sentence below. Find the error and circle it. Then correct the error in the blank under the sentence. The first one is done for you.

1. <u>Both</u> California and New York <u>have</u> big populations, but California is (more large) than New York <u>in area</u>.   _____larger_____

2. Spanish <u>speak</u> in Argentina, but <u>Portuguese is</u> the <u>language of Brazil</u>.   _____

3. If you <u>want</u> my <u>advice</u>, you <u>should better</u> study, or <u>you'll</u> never pass the test tomorrow.   _____

4. <u>It's</u> difficult to <u>believe</u>, but I <u>have been studied</u> Chinese for the <u>past two years</u>.   _____

5. After Paulina <u>took</u> a shower, combed <u>her</u> hair, and <u>made</u> her lunch, she <u>was going</u> to school.   _____

6. <u>The children</u> <u>were</u> <u>extreme anxious</u> to know who <u>the winner was</u>.   _____

7. Mary was <u>surprised</u> that the books <u>costed</u> $80.00. She expected <u>them</u> to be <u>much cheaper</u>.   _____

8. I think <u>you'll</u> like the car I <u>just bought</u>; <u>it's</u> the same color <u>to</u> Mario's.   _____

9. Your cousin is <u>old enough</u> to vote <u>in</u> the <u>upcoming</u> election, <u>doesn't he</u>?   _____

10. I know <u>from experience</u> that <u>the</u> grass will not grow in this yard if you <u>didn't water</u> it <u>frequently</u>.   _____

11. Chen <u>tripped</u> and <u>broke his</u> arm <u>while</u> he <u>was crossed</u> the street.   _____

12. You <u>must to be</u> at <u>least</u> 16 years old <u>to apply</u> for a license <u>in this state</u>.   _____

13. When <u>the girls and I</u> arrived <u>at</u> the theater, <u>the</u> movie <u>had already been started</u>.   _____

14. I <u>was used</u> to spend <u>a lot of</u> time <u>playing pool</u>, but now I have a full-time job, and that keeps me <u>pretty busy</u>.   _____

15. <u>Most of the people</u> in <u>this</u> room <u>speak</u> several languages <u>and I do so</u>.   _____

SKILL OBJECTIVES: Finding and correcting grammatical errors; preparing for standardized tests. Explain to students that this page reviews many of the grammatical structures taught so far in this book. Explain that this exercise is typical of many such exercises on standardized tests. Review item 1 with the class and be sure students understand why *more large* has been circled and *larger* has been written; emphasize that all items require both kinds of answers: the error circled and the correction written. Then assign the page for independent written work. Review all answers with the class, making sure that students can find all errors and correct them.

Dear Dot

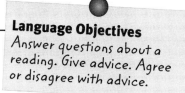

Language Objectives
Answer questions about a reading. Give advice. Agree or disagree with advice.

Dear Dot,

I will be graduating in June and am very confused about my future. I have been accepted at college and I want to go, but on the other hand I want to make some money and get into "the real world." I studied accounting in school, so I know I could get a job that pays fairly well. Should I get a job or should I continue with school? I'm not sure what I want to do at college, so I am leaning much more towards work. Please advise.

Graduate-to-be

Discuss each of the questions in class. Then write your answers.

1. What does "the real world" mean?

_____

2. What are the advantages of going to college?

_____

3. What are the advantages of going to work?

_____

4. What compromise solution can you suggest to Graduate-to-be?

_____

5. Do you think you will face the same problem when you finish high school? What decision do you think you will make? Why?

_____

Write About It

Now put yourself in Dot's place. Write a helpful answer to Graduate-to-be. Remember, you want to help solve the problem, not make fun of the writer or criticize.

Dear Graduate-to-be, _____

_____

_____

_____

_____

_____

SKILL OBJECTIVES: Interpreting figurative language; making judgments; drawing conclusions; expressing opinions in writing.
Have students read the letter. Discuss each question in class. Be sure students can support their opinions. This letter raises questions that are very important to students; allow ample time for the discussion. After students have written their answers to the questions, they can incorporate them in their letters.

Unit 8
Be a Good Sport

Gerunds: When Verbs Become Nouns

A gerund is a noun made out of a verb—a *verbal noun*. Gerunds are used as nouns, but they look exactly like present participles. Like present participles, they end in *-ing*. Like a noun, a gerund can be the subject of a sentence. It can also be used after a verb as the object of a sentence. Gerunds can be used with only certain verbs, however. With other verbs, it is necessary to use an infinitive instead of a gerund. Look at the two examples:

Jasmine avoids *exercising*.   (gerund)

Jasmine refuses *to exercise*.   (infinitive)

Look at the three boxes. The first box shows verbs that can be followed by a gerund. The second shows verbs that can be followed by either a gerund or an infinitive. The third shows verbs that can be followed only by an infinitive.

Gerund Only		Gerund or Infinitive		Infinitive Only	
admit	enjoy	begin	love	afford	hope
appreciate	finish	cease	neglect	agree	learn
avoid	mind	continue	prefer	choose	plan
consider	practice	hate	start	decide	refuse
deny	stop	like	try	forget	want

Complete the sentences using a gerund or an infinitive form of the verb in parentheses. The first two are done for you.

1. Lauri enjoys (play) _____playing_____ the violin.

2. Tomás and Maria like (dance) ____to dance____ .

3. Ronaldo started (take) _____ piano lessons two months ago.

4. Don't forget (do) _____ your homework.

5. I don't mind (do) _____ the laundry.

6. Do you want (have) _____ lunch with me today?

7. I'm glad that I've finally finished (paint) _____ the kitchen.

8. Where did you learn (play) _____ the guitar so well?

9. My mother hopes (return) _____ to her job soon.

10. Elena continued (talk) _____ even though Mrs. Sánchez asked her to stop.

11. Juan practices (speak) _____ English every day.

12. I can't afford (buy) _____ a Mercedes.

13. My sister prefers (read) _____ love stories instead of mysteries.

14. Paula hates (wash) _____ the dishes.

15. Will you consider (take) _____ this job?

16. I'd love (go) _____ with you if I could spare the time.

17. Vuong is planning (take) _____ a trip to San Francisco this spring.

18. You'll have to stop (make) _____ so much noise!

19. Jobida will begin (work) _____ in her new office next week.

20. Kate has chosen (continue) _____ her education after all.

SKILL OBJECTIVE: Choosing between gerunds and infinitives. Read the introductory paragraphs with the class, and make sure that students understand the difference between the two structures. Have students look at the three boxes, and give some examples: *I enjoy reading; I hate exercising* or *I hate to exercise; I hope to read that book.* Emphasize the importance of accurate usage in written and oral English. Then assign the items for independent written work.

Geruds and Prepositions

A gerund preceded by a preposition is a *gerund phrase*. Look at the example:

> Binh is interested *in going* to the pool today.

In the example, *in going* is a gerund phrase.

A Complete the gerund phrase in each of the following sentences by filling the blank with a gerund that makes sense in the sentence. The first one is done for you.

1. Thank you for _____coming_____ to my party.

2. Always wash your hands before _____ dinner.

3. I am interested in _____ to Disneyland.

4. Always look both ways before _____ the street.

5. Susanna is tired of _____ English.

6. Mr. Jones has been working at the bank for thirty years. Now he is 64 years old and is thinking about _____.

7. You should always read the directions on the container before _____ any medicine.

8. Do you have a recipe for _____ chocolate cake?

9. Before _____ the room, you should turn off all the lights.

10. Maria is thinking of _____ to Harvard University.

B Find a gerund that makes sense for each of the blanks, and write it in the blank.

Lari is a musician. She enjoys _____ many musical instruments. Lari started _____ the violin two years ago, but she began _____ piano lessons ten years ago when she was a little girl. She is also interested in _____ how to play the flute. _____ the piano and the violin every day takes a lot of time, however, so she thinks she'll wait another year before _____ flute lessons.

Lari likes _____ in New York City because she can go to lots of concerts. She prefers _____ to classical music, but she also enjoys _____ to jazz.

When Lari gets tired of _____ the violin and the piano, she likes _____ in the Palisades Interstate Park across the Hudson River from New York. Lately, Lari has been thinking about _____ to the Juilliard School of Music when she finishes high school.

C In your notebook, write the same three paragraphs about Lari, substituting infinitives for gerunds wherever you can.

SKILL OBJECTIVES: Using gerunds after prepositions; using gerunds and infinitives to complete sentences. Read the introductory material; be sure students understand what is meant by the term *gerund phrase*. *Part A:* Do the first three items orally; be sure students choose gerunds that make logical sense in the sentences, then assign as independent written work. *Part B:* Assign as written work, then have several students give their choices for the blanks. *Part C:* After this has been completed, go over it with the class.

Adjectives Ending in -ed and -ing

Some adjectives have two different forms. Look at the following examples:

confused → confusing   interested → interesting   excited → exciting

Adjectives ending in *-ing* usually express a person's opinion about something:

The speech was confus**ing**.   That subject is interest**ing**.   Your idea is excit**ing**.

Adjectives ending in *-ed* usually express an emotion, how someone feels:

I am very confus**ed**.   I am interest**ed** in that subject.   He was excit**ed** by my idea.

A **Circle the correct form of the adjective in each sentence. The first one is done for you.**

1. We were (surprised / surprising) when the rain started.

2. That movie was the most (amazed / amazing) film I've ever seen.

3. The news was (shocked / shocking).

4. The children were (stunned / stunning) when they found out.

5. That film was (frightened / frightening).

6. The accident was (horrified / horrifying) to see.

7. Emily was (embarrassed / embarrassing) when she spilled coffee on her blouse.

8. Skiing is an (excited / exciting) sport.

9. My mother was (pleased / pleasing) with her gift.

10. That TV program was the most (bored / boring) one I have ever seen.

11. Science is a (fascinated / fascinating) subject.

12. This book is the most (interested / interesting) one I have read in a long time.

13. The students were (relieved / relieving) when the test was canceled.

14. Vanya's report was very (confused / confusing); I didn't understand it at all.

15. The puppies were (terrified / terrifying) by the noise of the fireworks.

16. My sister felt (satisfied / satisfying) with her grades.

17. She is the most (bored / boring) teacher in school. I'm always (bored / boring) in her class.

18. Mr. Collins has a (surprised / surprising) number of books about World War II.

19. They have never been (interested / interesting) in learning about other cultures.

20. Of course we were very (disappointed / disappointing) to lose last night's game.

B **Now write a sentence in your notebook for each of the following words. Make sure you use them as adjectives. Do not copy any of the sentences in Part A.**

thrilled	astonished	bored	excited	tired
thrilling	astonishing	boring	exciting	tiring

SKILL OBJECTIVES: Using *-ed/ -ing* adjectives correctly; expanding vocabulary; differentiating between two forms of the same word. Explain that *-ed* and *-ing* words can be used as adjectives as well as verbs. Review the explanation at the top of the page and discuss the differences in meaning between the *-ed* and *-ing* forms of the same word. Then assign Part A for independent work. *Part B:* You may wish to have students write their sentences as homework.

What's the Sport?

Read the sentences at the left and decide which sport each one is telling about. Write the letter of that sport in the blank. Each sentence has one or more vocabulary clues to help you identify the sport. The first one is done for you.

Language Objective
Name sports activities from context clues.

1. Don't worry. You can buy new laces at the rink. _____k_____
2. Frank likes to do three miles a day. It usually takes him about 25 minutes. _____
3. The four friends picked up their racquets and went to the courts. _____
4. A sudden gust of wind caught the spinnaker and almost overturned the small boat. _____
5. The puck flew off the ice and into the stands. _____
6. I did twenty laps in the pool this morning. _____
7. Only the goalie can touch the ball with his hands. _____
8. Pull your bow back and aim for the dot right in the middle of the target. _____
9. Gerri dribbled quickly as she ran down the court. _____
10. After Ben knocked down all the pins, he won the match. _____
11. Back and forth the ball bounced on the table until finally Jane missed her shot and Rosie scored a point. _____
12. Mario ran down the track, leaned on his stick, and flew over the bar. _____
13. After Bruno got Wild Bill in a headlock, he threw him down on the mat, and the referee counted him out. _____
14. The white ball slammed into the 15 colored ones, and it was the 6 ball in the corner pocket and the 12 on the side. _____
15. After putting the bait on the line, you've got to sit in the boat and wait for a bite. _____
16. The players stood in a huddle and listened as the quarterback explained what to do. _____
17. All the fans had their eyes on the mound, waiting to see what the nervous pitcher would do. _____
18. Ramon stood at the top of the mountain. She dug her poles into the snow and pushed herself out and down. _____
19. Rick landed a quick right, a stinging left, and a couple of jabs, and his opponent was down, knocked out in the fourth round. _____
20. Adela swung her driver, and the little white ball sailed in the air and landed on the green. _____

a. bowling
b. basketball
c. hockey
d. soccer
e. wrestling
f. pole-vaulting
g. tennis
h. baseball
i. golf
j. fishing
k. skating
l. boxing
m. swimming
n. sailing
o. football
p. table tennis
q. archery
r. skiing
s. pool
t. jogging

SKILL OBJECTIVES: Classifying; using context clues; making inferences; interpreting figurative language. Read the directions at the top of the page. Ask students to underline the words in each example that are the context clues (e.g. *rink* in item 1). Allow time for students to read through both columns before attempting the matching exercise. If possible, do the page as a group activity to let students share their collective knowledge and find trickier answers by the process of elimination.

You've Got a Problem

Solve the following problems. Use your notebook to figure on if you need to. The first problem is done for you.

Language Objective
Solve mathematical word problems.

Your Answer

1. The Bullets have won half of their games this season. They have played 90 games so far. How many have they won?

___45___

2. To figure a batting average, divide the number of hits by the number of times a person has attempted to hit. Carry your division out to three decimal places. What is the batting average of a person who has hit:

   12 times in 60 attempts? _____
   15 times in 60 attempts? _____
   18 times in 59 attempts? _____
   33 times in 102 attempts? _____

3. If 579 fans paid $2.50 each to attend last week's basketball game at Dover Falls High School, how much money did the school take in that night?

_____

4. If one of the members of the swim team can swim 75 yards in one minute, how far can she swim in a quarter of an hour?

_____

5. Jules Lemmon, a professional football player, earned $450,000 in his first year as a pro. He earned $580,000 in his second year, $720,000 in his third, and $850,000 in his fourth year. In his fifth and final year as a player, Jules earned $970,000. What was his average salary for the five years that he was a professional player?

_____

6. While practicing for a race, a race-car driver drove steadily at 140 m.p.h. for thirty minutes. How far did he drive in that time?

_____

7. Molly ran the 100-yard dash in 17.26 seconds. Carmen ran it in 16.37 seconds. What was the difference in their times?

_____

8. A hockey player scores a point for each goal he makes. The player also scores a point for helping another player to make a goal (an assist). How many points does each of the following players have if they have made:

   35 goals and 39 assists? _____
   49 goals and 47 assists? _____
   46 goals and 61 assists? _____
   43 goals and 38 assists? _____

SKILL OBJECTIVE: Solving mathematical word problems. Ask students to read quickly through the problems and underline or circle any terms that are unfamiliar; explain these terms. Allow time for students to do the problems, then have volunteers put the math work on the board and let individual students explain their problem-solving methods. (Answers are on page 117.)

Adjective Form or Noun Form?

Language Objectives
Distinguish between adjective and noun forms to complete sentences. Write sentences to show the difference between a word's adjective and noun form.

Many words have similar adjective and noun forms. Look at the following examples:

different → difference   important → importance

impatient → impatience   distant → distance

Use the adjective form to tell which or what kind. Use adjectives before nouns or after forms of *to be*. See the sentences below:

We have different opinions about Joe.   Karen and I were silent in class.

Use the noun form to express the quality that someone or something has:

Identical twins have few physical differences.   Silence is required in the library.

A Circle the correct form in each sentence. (The adjective form is always first and the noun form is second.) The first one is done for you.

1. It is very ((important) / importance) to be on time.
2. José has only one (absent / absence) from school.
3. The man maintained his (innocent / innocence) throughout the trial.
4. (Adolescent / Adolescence) can be a difficult time of life.
5. You have to be very (patient / patience) to teach kindergarteners.
6. Many college students are (dependent / dependence) on the government for tuition money.
7. The view of the mountains was (magnificent / magnificence).
8. The (ignorant / ignorance) of the people was shocking.
9. If you look in the (distant / distance) you can see the sea.
10. The children were (confident / confidence) of winning.
11. The United States is (tolerant / tolerance) of all religions.
12. You mustn't be (negligent / negligence) about dental care.
13. Her (present / presence) at the party made it a success.
14. The boss fired the two (incompetent / incompetence) workers.
15. The United States declared its (independent / independence) from England in 1776.
16. The boy was (silent / silence) when the principal questioned him.
17. I'm (confident / confidence) that I'll do well on the test.
18. Her rudeness and (insolent / insolence) upset all of us.
19. The table was loaded with an (abundant / abundance) of food.
20. The President assured us he would be (present / presence) at the ceremony.

B Now write a sentence in your notebook for each of the following words. Do not copy any of the sentences in Part A. Use a dictionary if you need to.

dependent	important	reluctant	affluent	different
dependence	importance	reluctance	affluence	difference

SKILL OBJECTIVES: Choosing between adjective and noun forms; building vocabulary; internalizing grammar rules. Review the boxed explanation of adjectives and nouns at the top of the page. Make sure students understand the concept of nouns, pronouns, and adjectives. Do a few examples as a class, then assign students independent time to complete the page on their own. Review the page together, with students taking turns reading the complete sentences aloud and explaining their choices.

In the Newspaper: the Sports Pages

Language Objectives
Answer questions about a reading. Interpret and write colorful language in a sports article.

The sports pages of a newspaper bring together a variety of stories on many different sports. In the same issue of a newspaper, you might find stories on baseball, football, basketball, hockey, golf, tennis, swimming, or any other sport that is played in the newspaper's area. There may be stories about school sports, college sports, and professional sports. Often there are interviews with players or managers. There are also reports of games, races, or other contests that have just taken place. Sports writing is *idiomatic*. It is full of colorful images and slang expressions. Some people say that sports language is a language all its own.

Read the following article from the sports pages.

YELLOWJACKETS EDGE TIGERS ON LAST-SECOND BUZZER BEATER

Following a hard-fought contest in which there were numerous lead changes, Buzz Gordon sank a 3-point desperation shot into the basket at the buzzer to keep the win streak of the Yellowjackets. It was the tenth consecutive win of the season, coming at the expense of the disappointed Tigers.

The game was an exciting one, with the Yellowjackets taking the early lead, hitting a string of 2-point and 3-point field goals. As the game advanced, however, the Tigers' star point guard, Steve Casey, began to hit an array of 3-point shots, aided by the dazzling playmaking of his point guard, Speedy Jones. As the Yellowjackets' lead was whittled away, their coach Jim "Eagle" Eyers switched strategies. After putting their center, "Sky" Williams, into the line-up, the Yellowjackets again took charge. Sky was a dominating force, scoring dunk shots and controlling the rebounds.

To counter Eagle Eyers' move, the Tigers' coach, Bill Jenkins, resorted to a strategy calculated to foul Sky each time he put his hands on the ball. Sky, notoriously poor at shooting foul shots, began to miss time after time. With each miss, the Tigers closed the point gap. Coach Eyers was forced to take Sky out of the game.

With less than 30 seconds remaining in the game, a spectacular assist from Jones to Casey for a driving lay-up knotted the score at 62 points. The Yellowjackets had the ball with 22 seconds left on the clock. They continued to look for an opening, but the Tigers' defense held on. With five seconds left in the game, the Yellowjackets called time-out to set up the last play. The inbounds pass went to "Brick" Adams, the Yellowjackets' burly forward, who then handed off to Gordon, freeing him with a block on the Tigers' defense. As Gordon's shot sailed through the air, and as time ran out, a hush fell over the home crowd. The shot was good! Nothing but net! A deafening roar exploded from the crowd. The Yellowjackets' undefeated season was alive!

A **Answer these questions about the article.**

1. What sport is being described in the article? _____

2. Which team was the first to be in the lead? _____

3. What position does Steve Casey play and for which team? _____

4. Who was described as having "dazzling playmaking" ability? _____

(Go on to the next page.)

SKILL OBJECTIVES: Reading comprehension; understanding figurative language; understanding words through context. Read and discuss the introductory paragraphs. Emphasize and clarify the idea of idiomatic expressions. Have students read the article silently and underline or circle expressions, figurative language, and specialized sports terms (*point guard, field goal, dunk shots, etc.*) Lead a discussion on why sports have such appeal. What are the major sports in students' native countries?

5. What is the nickname for the coach of the Yellowjackets? _____

6. What phrase describes Sky's foul-shooting ability?

_____

7. What words does the writer use when Brick Adams throws to Gordon?

_____

8. What phrase does the writer use to describe what Gordon's last shot did?

_____

9. What do you think the phrase *nothing but net* means?

_____

10. What does the word *undefeated* mean in the sentence "The Yellowjackets' undefeated season was alive!"?

_____

B **Write a summary of the article using ordinary English.**

_____

_____

_____

_____

_____

_____

_____

_____

_____

_____

_____

C **Bring in a sports article from your local newspaper. Write questions about it similar to those in section A, and have a partner answer them. With your partner, make a brief dictionary of some of the colorful or idiomatic expressions in the article, giving their meaning in ordinary English.**

D **Go to a sports contest or game and write a description of it. Try to use colorful language to make the game "come alive" in the reader's mind. Test your readers after they have read your story to see how well they have understood what actually happened at the game or contest.**

SKILL OBJECTIVES: Drawing conclusions; locating specific information; using context clues. *Part A:* Assign the questions as independent written work, then discuss with the class. *Part B:* You may wish to post articles and questions on the bulletin board. Ask students for new expressions (and their meanings) that they found in their articles. *Part C:* Have each article read by several students, then discuss some of the common problems students faced in writing their articles—and their solutions.

Your Choice of Words

Each sentence contains a pair of blanks. Complete each sentence with the appropriate set of words. Use a dictionary if you need to. The first one is done for you.

1. I could _____barely_____ hear the announcer, so I ____turned up____ the volume on the television set.
   - **a.** quietly / opened
   - **b.** hugely / turned off
   - **c.** barely / turned up
   - **d.** nervously / answered

2. When people work in _____ conditions, it's not unusual for _____ to develop.
   - **a.** handsome / rivalries
   - **b.** crowded / tensions
   - **c.** perfect / imperfections
   - **d.** dark / delight

3. The _____ who performed that operation was recently _____ as the top doctor in the tri-state region.
   - **a.** surgeon / honored
   - **b.** candidate / elected
   - **c.** nurse / fired
   - **d.** veteran / awarded

4. _____ people have been injured at this intersection that a new traffic light will be _____ as soon as possible.
   - **a.** Too many / ignored
   - **b.** So many / installed
   - **c.** Such / destroyed
   - **d.** How many / broken

5. The farmers are expecting a below-normal _____ due to the _____ rainfall this year.
   - **a.** harvest / sparse
   - **b.** farm / disorganized
   - **c.** animal / abundant
   - **d.** production / wet

6. There was a _____ feeling at the factory after the news of the closing was _____.
   - **a.** cheery / described
   - **b.** consistent / rejected
   - **c.** melancholy / announced
   - **d.** peculiar / translated

7. _____ several months of hard work, Jacob's entry in the Science Fair did not win any of the _____ prizes.
   - **a.** For / final
   - **b.** Despite / major
   - **c.** Because of / influential
   - **d.** Just as / important

8. The jury listened _____ while the defense lawyer presented her _____ remarks.
   - **a.** haphazardly / unkind
   - **b.** thoroughly / irrelevant
   - **c.** attentively / opening
   - **d.** friendly / remarkable

9. Gardening is a relaxing _____ for Mrs. Sánchez who has a stressful job as a stockbroker in a _____ Wall Street company.
   - **a.** job / corporate
   - **b.** portrait / growing
   - **c.** flowers / leading
   - **d.** hobby / large

SKILL OBJECTIVES: Understanding vocabulary in context; preparing for standardized tests. Explain to students that this type of exercise is similar to those found on some standardized tests. Explain that they must read each sentence completely—both the words before and those after the blanks—in order to get an idea of what the sentence is saying and thus know which pair of words to pick. Warn students that they must use both words in a single pair—they cannot use one word from one pair and another from a second pair. Discuss the first item and be sure students understand why pair c was chosen. Then assign the page for independent written work.

Dear Dot

Dear Dot,
   Vacation is coming, and I dread it. Everyone starts playing sports, and I am no good at any of them. I have to stay at home or just watch from the sidelines. I would love to play, but I am a first-class klutz, and I never can seem to do the right thing when I am playing any sport. In school when I have to play I am always the last one picked for any team. Is there anything I can do to improve my sports ability?
                                                    Loser

Discuss each of the questions in class. Then write your answers.

1. What is a *klutz*? _____

_____

2. How does a person become good at anything? _____

_____

3. What is *confidence*? Is confidence important in sports? _____

_____

4. How can Loser change? _____

_____

Write About It

Now put yourself in Dot's place. Write a helpful answer to Loser. Remember, you want to help solve the problem, not make fun of the writer or criticize.

Dear Loser, _____

_____

_____

_____

_____

_____

_____

_____

                                        _____

SKILL OBJECTIVES: Reading for main idea; understanding figurative language; making judgments; expressing opinions in writing. Have students read the letter. Review the questions orally, and encourage as much dialogue as possible; be sure students support their opinions. Then have students write answers to the questions. Suggest they use these answers as the basis for their letters. You may wish to assign the letter-writing activity as homework.

Language Objectives
Answer questions about a reading. Interpret a cartoon's meaning.

Read the article.

The word *tax* is one of the easiest of English words to read. But it is one of the most difficult to explain in English or in any other language. Taxes are a complicated topic about which many people's opinions differ.

In 1776, when people in the United States were struggling to plan a new country, taxes were talked about a lot. Money to run the government had to be raised somehow. That year, the Scottish economist Adam Smith published a very long book titled *The Wealth of Nations*. In it he described taxes in a few short lines. He gave four rules that he said should be followed by any nation—old or new.

Here are Adam Smith's four rules, slightly changed to more modern English:

I. The citizens of every country ought to give money towards the support of the government, as nearly as possible, in proportion to the monies which they have earned because their country protects them.

II. The tax which each individual must pay ought to be certain, and not guessed at. The time of payment, the manner of payment, the amount to be paid, ought all to be clear and plain to the citizen who has to pay it, and to every other person.

III. Every tax ought to be set by law at the time, or in the way, in which it is most convenient for the citizen to pay it.

IV. Every tax ought to be planned so taxes pay what the country needs and not a lot more than the country really needs.

Thirteen years later Benjamin Franklin wrote in a letter to a friend:

Our Constitution is in actual operation; everything appears to promise that it will last; but in this world nothing is certain but death and taxes.

Things may have changed since Adam Smith and Benjamin Franklin gave their opinions about taxes. But taxes are still part of everyday life.

Today almost everyone pays taxes. They pay directly in income taxes or indirectly in sales and other taxes. Most people understand that a country must be supported by the citizens who live there. Some people pay their taxes gladly. Some people think they pay too much in taxes. Some people try not to pay taxes at all.

Most citizens have strong feelings about taxes. They try to vote for state and national representatives who will pass reasonable tax laws.

(Go on to the next page.)

SKILL OBJECTIVES: Reading for details; building vocabulary; understanding taxes. Have students read the page and discuss it. Make sure students understand that Adam Smith and Benjamin Franklin were famous writers who, like many people, had strong opinions about taxes.

Write *True* after each statement that agrees with the passage you read. Write *False* if the statement does not agree with what the passage states.

1. Taxes are monies that governments get from their citizens. _____

2. People have different opinions about taxes. _____

3. Adam Smith said that the amount of tax money a person has to pay should be certain and not just guessed at. _____

4. Benjamin Franklin said that he thought the Constitution was working well so far. _____

B **Choose one paragraph from the passage you read and write your opinion of it or what you think it means in your own words.**

_____

_____

_____

_____

_____

_____

_____

_____

C **What do you think this cartoon means?**

SKILL OBJECTIVES: Reading for details; building vocabulary; distinguishing between true/false statements. Review the concept of taxes. *Part A:* Use the passages on page 82 to determine the veracity of the four statements. *Part B:* Choose one paragraph and write an opinion about it. *Part C:* Discuss possible meanings of the cartoon. Ask students if they agree with the point of view of the cartoonist.

A State Income Tax Form

Every April, people who work in the United States have to report how much they have earned to the Department of Taxation and Finance for their state. A State Income Tax Form is shown below. This form can be picked up at a bank or a post office. Use this filled in form to answer questions on page 85. It is the first page of a New York State Income Tax Form.

A Look at this State Income Tax Form.

New York State Department of Taxation and Finance

Resident Fast Form Income Tax Return
New York State • City of New York • City of Yonkers

2003 IT-100

For office use only

Important: You must enter your social security number(s) in the boxes to the right.

Your first name and middle initial	Your last name *(for a joint return, enter spouse's name on line below)*
Iam J	Everybody
Spouse's first name and middle initial	Spouse's last name

Your social security number: 555-61-777
Spouse's social security number:

Mailing address *(number and street or rural route)*: 169 Pleasant Place
Apartment number: 47
NY State county of residence: • New York

City, village, or post office: New York
State: NY
ZIP code: 17432
School district name: : Yorky

Permanent home address *(see instructions) (number and street or rural route)*: Same
Apartment number: Same
School district code number: 000

City, village, or post office: Same
State: NY
ZIP code: Same

(A) Filing status — mark an X in one box:
① ☒ Single
② ☐ Married filing joint return
③ ☐ Head or household *(with qualifying person)*
④ ☐ Qualifying widow(er) with dependent child

(B) Can you be claimed as a dependent on another taxpayer's federal return? .... Yes ☐ No ☒

(C) Were you a city of New York resident for all of 2003? *(Part-year residents must file Form IT-201; see instructions.)* .... Yes ☒ No ☐

(D) Were you a city of Yonkers resident for all of 2003? *(Part-year residents must file Form IT-201; see instructions.)* .... Yes ☐ No ☒

1 Number of federal exemptions *(1040EZ filers - enter "1" if single, "2" if married; 1040A filers - copy from line 6d. We will figure your New York State dependent exemptions for you.)* **1.** 1

If any of the entries on lines 2 through 7 below will be $100,000 or greater, stop; you cannot use From IT-100.

		Dollars	Cents
2	Wages, salaries, tips, etc. *(1040EZ filers - copy from line 1; 1040A filers - copy from line 7)*	**2.** 50,000	00
3	Taxable interest income *(1040EZ filers - copy from line 2; 1040A filers - copy from line 8a)*	**3.** 123	00
4	Interest income on U.S. government bonds included on line 3 above	**4.** 200	00
5	Ordinary dividends *(1040EZ filers - enter "0"; 1040A filers - copy from line 9a)*	**5.** 110	00
6	Unemployment compensation *(1040EZ filers - copy from line 3; 1040A filers - copy from line 13)*	**6.** 100	00
7	Individual retirement arrangement (IRA) deduction *(1040EZ filers - enter "0"; 1040A filers- copy from line 17)*	**7.** —	—

8 **Voluntary gifts/contributions** *(whole dollar amounts only; see instructions)* Olympic Fund .... ☐ o.
Return a Gift to Wildlife... ☐ w.   Breast Cancer Research Fund ... ☐ b.
Missing/Exploited Children Fund ... ☐ c.   Alzheimer's Fund ... ☐ a.

9 Amount of federal earned income credit *(see instructions and complete the back of this form)* ...... **9.** — 00

10 Amount of federal child and dependent care credit *(see instructions and complete the back of this form)* ...... **10.** — 00

Lines 11, 12, and 13 —Tax withheld *(from your wage and tax statement(s))*

New York State **11.** 12,252.67   City of New York **11.** 2,000.00   City of Yonkers **13.**

For office use only

Third – party designee Do you want to allow another person to discuss this return with the Tax Dept? *(see instructions)* ☐ Yes *(complete the following)* ☐ No
Designee's name | Designee's phone number | Personal identification number (PIN)

Paid preparer's use only
Prepare's signature | Prepare's SSN or PTIN
Firm's name *(or yours, if self-employed)* | Employer identification number
Address | Date | Mark X if self-employed ☐

Sign your return here
Your signature: Iam J. Everybody
Spouse's signature *(if joint return)*
Date: 4/3/04 | Daytime phone number (optional)

001394   Mail to: STATE PROCESSING CENTER, PO BOX 61000, ALBANY NY 12261-0001   IT-100 2003

(Go on to the next page.)

Answer the following questions, using the information in the form on page 84. Use complete sentences. The first question has been answered for you.

1. What is the name of the person filling out this form?

   His name is Iam J. Everybody.

2. What street does Iam live on?

   _____

3. What is Iam's zip code?

   _____

4. Is Iam married?

   _____

5. How many federal exemptions did Iam have?

   _____

6. What were Iam's wages in 2003?

   _____

7. According to line 6, how much unemployment compensation did Iam get?

   _____

8. Did Iam have more dividends or taxable interest income?

   _____

9. How much did Iam give to Return a Gift to Wildlife?

   _____

10. Did Iam have any City of Yonkers tax withheld from his paycheck?

    _____

11. On what date did Iam sign his tax return?

    _____

12. How much New York State tax was withheld from Iam's paycheck?

    _____

13. Can Iam be claimed as a dependent?

    _____

14. Was Iam a resident of the city of New York for the whole year?

    _____

15. To what city in New York is the form supposed to be mailed when it is complete?

    _____

SKILL OBJECTIVE: Read a filled-out form to answer questions about it.

85

In the Newspaper: Help Wanted

Language Objectives
Answer questions about Help Wanted ads. Take part in a mock job interview. Write a sample resume and cover letter.

The Help Wanted (job) ads are found in the Classified section of the newspaper, along with real estate listings, apartments for rent, second-hand car listings, and ads for other things people want to sell. Help Wanted ads are often divided into several categories, for example, Education, Finance, Healthcare, Sales, Technology. As you read the Help Wanted ads below, decide under which heading each belongs.

OFFICE ASSISTANT

Full-time opportunity to work in warm, friendly but busy lawyer's office in San Diego Central Business District. You will help with filing, answering the telephone, etc. Requires high school education, pleasant personality, computer skills + willingness to work at varied duties. Salary open. Please send resume to jfoster@legaleagles.org.

ESL Instructors

F.T./P.T. Days/Eves.
(1) Attleboro/Fall River, two full-time positions, available now.
(2) Various Southeast CA locations, part-time. Email resumes to fricardoHR @urbanistics.com.

RETAIL: INFANT TO TEEN

A BETTER CHILDREN'S APPAREL STORE

STORE MANAGERS
ASSISTANT MANAGERS
SALESPERSONS

Top salary and benefits for the qualified. Send resume to

LITTLE FOLKS SHOP
Div. ABC Shoe Corp.
Executive Office
Rte. 337
Charlesville, IL 69999

AUTOMOTIVE CAREERS

You must be able to work in a progressive, fast-moving automotive service organization. We need mature, serious, professional, responsible hard workers with strong desire to succeed to work as Service Advisors. Must enjoy customer contact & technical decision making. Contact for appointment Roy Chevrolet, Rte. 114, Denville.

Data Entry

Wrightsville's Phelps Press seeks 2 exp. desktop operators to process text of current books and magazines and translate them into Braille on our specialized computer system. Requirements are exc. typing and spelling, proficiency with the English language and an interest in learning Braille. Good benefits. Starting salary $25,000-30,000. Email resume to: jones@seeingeyepress.com

TELLERS

Work on beautiful Cape Cod in a new community Federal Credit Union. Excellent salary and benefits. Please send resume to:
FEDERAL CREDIT UNION
Box 62, Cape Cod, MA.

RENTAL AGENT

Part-time energetic Rental Agent wanted for a fast-growing development. Please send resume to:
BELPORT HISTORIC ASSOCIATION, 100 Captains Row, Belport.

Computer Sales

Dale City area. Join the world's fastest growing chain of retail computer stores. You must be a sales pro with superior communication skills. Accounting, small-business or computer background helpful, but not required. College degree a must. Earning potential unlimited. We are a people-oriented company with excellent benefits. Email resumes to **helenwood@computercity.com**. **No phone calls.**

PRODUCTION INVENTORY CONTROL CLERK

Well estab. manufacturer & distributor. Immed. opening. Growth oppty to also learn purchasing. Accuracy w/ details & figures a must. Email resume to: gstanley@V88Times.com.

Training Opportunity for
NURSE AIDS
7–3:30 Only

Six-month training program. Upon completion, certificate issued & full-time permanent position. 40 hours weekly & benefits. Send resume and cover letter to:

PERSONNEL OFFICE
ELIHU WAITE NURSING & REHABILITATION CENTER
HARRIS COVE 92931

A Some job advertisements ask applicants to call for an interview appointment. Others ask applicants to send or email a resume (rez'e mā) explaining their background and qualifications for the job. The employer looks through all the resumes, selects the best qualified applicants, and then asks those people to come in for a personal interview. At the interview, the employer asks questions such as those below.

Choose a Help Wanted ad from above that interests you. In your notebook, write answers to the questions below. For item 6, feel free to ask the employer any questions you'd like answered. Next, practice the interview with a partner. Your partner, who is playing the employer, must answer the questions you ask in item 6.

1. Why are you interested in this job?

2. Have you ever had a job before? If so, what was it?

3. What special qualifications do you have for this job?

4. What are you doing at present?

5. When could you begin this job?

6. Are there any questions you'd like to ask me about this job?

(Go on to the next page.)

SKILL OBJECTIVES: Reading for detail; classifying; interpreting Help Wanted ads; role playing. Read and discuss the introductory paragraph. Give students time to read the ads, then discuss the heading under which each would be found. *Part A:* If possible, allow each student to role play both the employer's and the employee's part. Individuals who feel confident about their English may perform their interviews for the class.

B

A resume gives concise information about your background, your work experience, your job education, and your interests. The information on the resume will help you fill out the job application forms. It is important that your resume is neat and well organized, and that the information is easy to read.

Look at the resume at the right. Notice how Andrea has set up the resume and the type of information she has given. Choose a Help Wanted ad from page 86 that interests you. In your notebook, write your own resume, following the format shown here. Under Experience, list your most recent job first. Under Education, list your most recent school first.

Andrea Villarosa
769 Everett Street
San Diego, California 92110
Telephone: 441-8864
avillarosa@mailnet.com

Position Desired:	**Office Assistant**	
Experience:	**Clerk**	Summers
	Milton Hospital	2002–2003
	San Diego, CA	
	Child Care Assistant	After school
	Care4Kids Childcare Center	2001–2004
	323 San Mateo Rd.	
	San Diego, CA	
	Library assistant (volunteer)	1999–2000
	Central Middle School	
	San Diego, CA	
Education:	San Diego High School	2001–2004
	(Commercial course)	
	Central Middle School	1998–2001
	San Diego, CA	
	South Central Elementary	1991–1998
Special Abilities:	Bilingual in Spanish and English	
	Proficient in Excel and Powerpoint	
Awards and Activities	"Outstanding Business Student"	2004
	Captain, Girl's Basketball Team	2003–2004
	President, Debate Team	2002–2004

C

When you send a resume, you also have to send a cover letter to introduce yourself and interest your potential employer. Study the sample cover letter at the right. In your notebook, write a similar cover letter to go with your resume. Tell your potential employer which job you are applying for and briefly mention your strongest qualifications. Before closing, express your interest in meeting for an interview.

---

769 Everett Street
San Diego, California 92110

June 15, 2004

Ms. Joan Foster
Computacorp
22 Main Street
San Diego, California 92109

Dear Ms. Foster,

I am answering your ad in the *Patriot Herald* for the position of Office Assistant. I am graduating from San Diego High School this month. I was just named "Outstanding Business Student." My previous work experience includes two summers as a clerk at Milton Hospital and after-school Assistant at the Care4Kids Childcare Center. I enjoy office work and working with people very much.

I would like to come in and talk with you about the position. I am enclosing my resume with more information about myself.

Sincerely,

Andrea Villarosa

Andrea Villarosa

SKILL OBJECTIVES: Writing a resume; writing a cover letter. Read and discuss the first two paragraphs. Emphasize the importance of neatness and accuracy in a resume. Discuss the term "cover letter" (also called covering letter) and stress that this, too, must be neat and correctly phrased and spelled. Elicit that a carelessly prepared resume or letter suggests that the applicant may be generally careless and may lose him or her a job. Then assign Parts B and C. Have students exchange and discuss their resumes and letters.

Figure It Out!

Read the problems below, then answer the questions. Use the space provided on the right to do the necessary math work. The first one is done for you.

1. You and your friend are in a restaurant in Boston. Your bill comes to $50.00. In Massachusetts, there is a 5% meal tax on restaurant meals.

   a. How much meal tax must you pay? _____ $2.50 _____

   b. What will the total bill be? _____ $52.50 _____

   $$
   \begin{array}{ll}
   \$50 & \text{(bill)} \\
   \times.05 & \text{(x5\%)} \\
   \hline
   \$2.50 & = \text{meal tax}
   \end{array}
   $$

2. You are in the same restaurant in Boston. This time your bill, including the meal tax, comes to $82.00. Usually, people leave their waitress or waiter a 15% tip.

   a. How much tip should you leave? _____

   b. How much will you spend on the meal, including the tip? _____

3. George's godmother has just left him $4,000 in her will. In Oregon, where George lives, the state charges a 12% inheritance tax.

   a. How much tax must George pay? _____

   b. How much money will he have left after paying the inheritance tax? _____

4. Mr. Pappas bought a new Ford Focus last month. He paid $15,500 for it. Mr. Pappas lives in a state where the sales tax is 8%.

   a. How much sales tax did he pay? _____

   b. What was the total cost of the car? _____

5. Mrs. Gonzales makes $62,000 a year. This year, all wage owners must pay 6.2% of their salary to Social Security. How much will Mrs. Gonzales pay towards Social Security this year?

   _____

6. Carolina took a taxi from the airport to her apartment. The price was $25.50. People usually figure a 15% tip for the driver, add the tip to the fee, then pay the driver the nearest round amount. How much did Carolina probably give the driver?

   _____

7. Mr. and Mrs. Ayala own a house in Rexford. The value of the house is $210,000. The property tax in Rexford is 2.5% of the property value. How much do the Ayalas pay in property taxes every year?

   _____

Finding a Job

Here are some more Help Wanted ads. These jobs were listed in the Classified section under the heading "General Help." Read the ads, then answer the questions below.

Language Objective
Answer questions about Help Wanted ads.

AUTOPARTS COUNTER PERSON
Must be experienced. Alltown area. 379-0065. Ask for Joe.

CLERK   Bilingual, must be fast, accurate typist. Good phone personality with Spanish/English customers. Excellent benefits. Send resume to JillWagner@hispanicnews.com.

COUNTER PERSON   Dry cleaning store. Full-time 7–3. 337-4445.

DELIVERY/MESSENGER   Person with own car to work for downtown law firm. $375/wk + travel expenses. Call Office Manager, 758-0722.

DESK CLERK   All shifts, full- and part-time. Brewster Hotel. Call Jean Stall, 734-6672.

NEWSPAPER CARRIERS   Openings for permanent part-time carriers M–F, 4 a.m.–8 a.m. Must have reliable vehicle. Salary $7.50 per hr. Please call btwn 8 a.m. and noon only for appt. 333-1218.

MECHANICS   Dealership needs mechanics for day and night shifts. Excellent pay and benefits. For information, stop in. Ask for Service Manager. Allen's Ford, 40 Jay St., Newtown.

SECURITY GUARDS   Full- and part-time in and around Newtown area. Many positions available. Must be 21 yrs. or over with a H.S. diploma. danamici@alphasecurity.com.

SERVICE STATION ATTENDANT   Clean, neat, personable. Apply Wed. May 14, 520 Northover Pike, Lincoln.

TRAVEL AGENT   for our Eastwood office. Computer knowledge and excellent phone manner essential. Please send resumes to DanFerris@ApexTravel.com.

A

1. Name two jobs you can apply for by email. _____

2. Name two jobs for which you need your own car. _____

3. Name one job requiring computer knowledge. _____

4. Name one job for which you must be a high school graduate. _____

5. What type of work would the dry cleaning counter person do? _____

6. What sort of experience would the autoparts counter person need? Why? _____

7. What would the duties of the hotel desk clerk be? _____

8. What would the duties of the security guard be? _____

B

Many of these ads ask you to call for an interview appointment. When you call, the employer will probably ask you some questions over the phone. Choose one job to call for an interview. Complete the conversation below in your notebook, then practice the telephone dialogue with a partner.

Employer: Hello, this is _____. Can I help you?

You:

Employer: Do you have any work experience?

You:

Employer:

You:

Employer: Can you begin work immediately?

You:

Employer: When can you come in for an interview?

You:

Employer: All right. Thank you for calling. We'll see you then.

SKILL OBJECTIVES: Reading for specific information; interpreting Help Wanted ads; role playing. Allow time for students to read the ads. *Part A:* Do the first two questions with the class, then assign for independent written work. *Part B:* Have students complete the dialogue individually, then work in pairs practicing both dialogues. Ask for volunteers to role play their dialogues for the class.

Preparing for Tests: Stated and Implied Ideas (2)

Language Objective
Answer questions about a reading.

Read the article.

Alaska, the largest state in the United States, is more than twice the size of Texas, the second largest state. Alaska is separated from the state of Washington by about 500 miles of Canadian land.

Tsar Peter the Great of Russia wanted to find out if Asia and North America were connected by land. In 1725, he sent Vitus Bering, a Danish sea captain, to explore the North Pacific region.

In 1741, Bering led a second expedition to the area. He saw the North American mainland, and landed on Kayak Island.

Russia established a settlement in Alaska, on Kodiak Island, in 1784, and later claimed Alaska for Russia. When Russians first arrived in Alaska, three groups of native North Americans were living there—the Eskimos, the Aleuts, and the Indians. Russian fur traders made slaves of some of them and treated most of the others badly.

In 1867, the United States Secretary of State William H. Seward bought Alaska from Russia for $7,200,000—about 2 cents an acre. Many people in the United States thought it was worth less than that and called the purchase Seward's Folly (foolish mistake).

Congress did not provide for an Alaskan government for the next seventeen years. Alaska was managed first by the U.S. War Department, then by the Treasury Department, and then by the Navy Department.

In 1912, Congress established Alaska as a U.S. territory. Congress approved Alaskan statehood on June 30, 1958.

On January 3, 1959, President Dwight D. Eisenhower proclaimed Alaska the forty-ninth state—the first new state in forty-seven years.

Circle the best answer for each question.

1. Peter the Great sent Vitus Bering to explore the North Pacific region because
   a. Bering was the captain of a large kayak.
   b. he wanted to discover Denmark.
   c. he wanted to find out if Asia and North America were connected by land.
   d. he was looking for Texas.

2. Russian settlement in Alaska was
   a. helpful to the natives living there.
   b. harmful to the Russian fur traders who became slaves.
   c. governed by William H. Seward.
   d. harmful to the native population of Alaska.

3. The U.S. Treasury Department managed Alaska
   a. after the War Department.
   b. after the Navy Department.
   c. before the War Department.
   d. for seventeen years.

4. Which of the following represents a logical conclusion about the purchase of Alaska from Russia?
   a. The Russians asked for too much money for Alaska.
   b. The purchase of Alaska was good for the United States.
   c. Seward made a foolish mistake.
   d. The native population of Alaska finally got their land back.

SKILL OBJECTIVES: Reading for inference; finding specific information; drawing conclusions. Explain to students that this exercise is typical of those found on standardized tests. Remind them of the importance of reading carefully but quickly. You may want to give them a time limit—six minutes is suggested—to accustom them to pacing themselves. After they have completed the exercise, reread the passage orally and have students take turns answering the questions; discuss/explain all answers, paying special attention to the inference questions.

Dear Dot

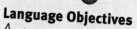

Dear Dot,
    I am a boy and I would like to be a nurse. I don't tell many people that because even my closest friends laugh at me when I tell them, but it is true. My uncle is a male nurse and he is a nice guy and his job sounds great. I want to be like him, and I want to be part of the medical profession. Even my family says that I should try to be a doctor, but that's not what I want. I want to be a nurse. What can I tell my friends and family so that they will leave me alone?

                                            Bugged

Discuss each of the questions in class. Then write your answers.

1. Why do people laugh when Bugged says he wants to be a nurse? _____

_____

2. Do you think there is such a thing as a woman's profession or a man's profession?
Why or why not? _____

_____

3. What are the advantages of being a nurse rather than a doctor? _____

_____

4. Do you think Bugged's family should try to persuade him to be a doctor? Why or why not?

_____

5. What can Bugged say to the people who question his career choice? _____

_____

Write About It

Now put yourself in Dot's place. Write a helpful answer to Bugged. Remember, you want to help solve the problem, not make fun of the writer or criticize him.

Dear Bugged, _____

_____

_____

_____

_____

                                            _____

SKILL OBJECTIVES: Reading for main idea and details; making inferences and judgments; expressing opinions in writing. Read the letter aloud (or have a student read it). Discuss each question in class. Encourage freedom of expression, but be sure students can support their opinions. Then have students write answers to the questions. Suggest they use these answers as the basis for their letters. You may wish to assign the letter-writing activity as homework.

Language Objective
Express contrary-to-fact wishes and statements.

A Sonya and Raul recently moved from Santo Domingo to St. Paul, Minnesota. They are having some problems in their new surroundings.

1. They can't find good jobs.
2. They can't get used to American food.
3. They can't make any new friends.
4. They can't speak English well.
5. They can't get used to the cold weather.

Sonya and Raul wish that they could do all these things. If they could, they would be much happier. Look at the five problems listed above. What do Sonya and Raul wish they could do? Answer with five complete sentences. The first one is done for you.

1. _They wish that they could find good jobs._
2. _____
3. _____
4. _____
5. _____

B Here are some other problems that Sonya and Raul are having.

1. They don't have much money.
2. They don't have a car.
3. There isn't much heat in their apartment.
4. Their upstairs neighbors are very noisy.
5. They have a very small apartment.

What do Sonya and Raul wish? Answer with five complete sentences. Use the past tense for the second verb. The first one is done for you.

1. _They wish that they had more money._
2. _____
3. _____
4. _____
5. _____

C Complete the following sentences, using *would* or *could*. The first two are done for you. Use them as models.

1. If Sonya and Raul could find good jobs, _they would have more money._
2. If they spoke better English, _they could make more friends._
3. If they had a car, _____.
4. If they could figure out the money system, _____.
5. If they had a bigger apartment, _____.
6. If their upstairs neighbors were quieter, _____.

SKILL OBJECTIVES: Using *wish* conditional; completing conditional sentences. Write *They can't find good jobs.* on the board; under it write *They wish that they could find good jobs.* Discuss the structural changes and the change in verb tense; do the same with the first sentence of Part B, then assign both parts for independent written work. *Part C:* Discuss the difference in meaning between *could* and *would*; elicit that either one may fit in some sentences. Then assign as written work.

Mrs. Madison

Mrs. Madison is mad at everyone and everything. Why is she mad? Well, . . .

- Her daughter never cleans her bedroom.

- Her son spends too much time on his computer.

- Her husband works until 9 p.m. every night.

- Her sister calls her three times a day.

- It's been raining for six days.

It's too much!

A **What does Mrs. Madison wish? Answer in complete sentences. The first one is done for you.**

1. _She wishes that her daughter would clean her bedroom._

2. _____

3. _____

4. _____

5. _____

B **Who do you get mad at? What do you wish they would do? What do you wish they wouldn't do?**

1. _____

2. _____

3. _____

C **Read the situations below. What do these people wish that they had done? Answer the questions with complete sentences. Use the past perfect tense in your answer. The first one is done for you. Use it as a model.**

1. Sadie always spent her babysitting earnings on clothes, and never <u>saved</u> any money. Now she can't afford to go on the class trip to New York City.

   What does she wish? _She wishes that she had saved her money._

2. Daniel never studied much when he was in high school. He was not accepted at any of the colleges he applied to.

   What does he wish now? _____

3. Rosa and her husband went to France last month. They didn't take any French lessons before they went, and couldn't communicate with anyone.

   What do they wish they'd one? _____

   _____

SKILL OBJECTIVES: Using *wish* conditional with past and past perfect tenses; expressing wishes in writing. Read the anecdotal passage with the class. Make sure students understand the directions for Part A. Review the structural changes in the sample sentence, then assign. *Part B:* Discuss what students get mad at. Elicit sample answers; assign as written work. *Part C:* Note the tense shift from past to past perfect in the sample sentence *never saved; wishes that she had saved.* Assign as written work.

What Did You Say?

Language Objective
Use correct pronoun forms and verb structures to express reported speech.

A Answer the questions below. The first one is done for you. Notice that the verb *will* in the quoted speech is changed to *would* in the reported speech.

1. Martha said, "I <u>will</u> meet you in the cafeteria."

   What did she say? _She said that she would meet me in the cafeteria._

2. Paul and Ronnie said, "We will come to the party."

   What did they say? _____

3. My father said, "I will be in Washington, D.C., next week."

   What did he say? _____

4. The President said, "We must not let the terrorists win."

   What did he say? _____

5. The teacher said, "I will give you a test next Monday."

   What did she say? _____

6. I said, "I will pay the rent next week."

   What did I say? _____

7. We said, "We will take care of everything."

   What did we say? _____

B Answer the questions below. The first one is done for you. Notice that the past tense or present perfect verb in the quoted speech is changed to the past perfect in the reported speech.

1. My sister said, "I <u>saw</u> that movie last week."

   What did she say? _She said that she had seen that movie last week._

2. The weather reporters said, "The weather was sunny all last week."

   What did they say? _____

3. The newscaster said, "The police caught the robber."

   What did she say? _____

4. The teacher said, "I forgot to correct your homework."

   What did he say? _____

5. The President said, "I have reduced taxes."

   What did he say? _____

6. They said, "We have already eaten dinner."

   What did they say? _____

7. You said, "I have finally finished doing my homework."

   What did you say? _____

SKILL OBJECTIVE: Reported speech with past and perfect tenses. Discuss the difference between direct quotation and reported speech (indirect quotation). Point out the grammatical change from *will* to *would* (Part A), and from simple past to past perfect (Part B). Do the entire page orally with the class before assigning as independent written work.

Too, Very, Enough

Three frequently used words in English sentences are *too*, *very*, and *enough*. Look at the following sentence to see how each is used: "Martha was very tall, tall enough to stand out in a crowd, and too tall to wear most of the clothes in the store." Read the information in the chart.

Very	*Very* is called an intensifier because it intensifies (makes stronger) the word that follows it.
	Example: She was intelligent. She was very intelligent.
Too	*Too* is also an intensifier, but it goes beyond *very*. *Too* means more than is wanted or needed.
	Example: He is too young to go to school.
	This means that he is younger than is allowed to start school. *Too* gives a negative meaning to a sentence. "Too young to go to school" means one can't go to school.
Enough	*Enough* means the right amount. In these two sentences, *enough* modifies nouns.
	Example: There's enough food for everyone. We don't have enough time.

Enough **can also modify or change the meaning of adjectives. When you use an adjective +** *enough* **+ an infinitive, you are saying that something is possible—that it can be done.**

Example: He is tall enough to play basketball.

When *enough* **is used to modify an adjective in a negative statement, it has the opposite meaning: something is impossible, cannot be done.**

Example: He is not tall enough to play basketball.

Complete the sentences. Use *too, very*, or *enough*.

1. Mr. Smith is 84; he's _____ old to find a job.

2. Mrs. Getty is rich _____ to buy anything she wants.

3. Do you have _____ money to buy that bicycle?

4. San Francisco is a _____ beautiful city.

5. My daughter is _____ young to drive a car.

6. Susanna can't play basketball because she's _____ short.

7. George is 18. Is he old _____ to get married?

8. I am _____ sorry to hear about your accident.

9. Miami is _____ nice, but it is _____ hot in the summer.

10. I don't like living in Canada; it's _____ cold.

11. There wasn't _____ snow, so we couldn't go skiing.

12. My car is _____ beautiful, but it uses _____ much gasoline.

13. Jesiquita is smart _____ to go to any college she wants.

14. I don't have _____ energy to go jogging today.

15. Chinese is a _____ difficult language to learn.

16. My father was _____ sick to go to work yesterday.

17. It isn't warm _____ to go to the beach today.

SKILL OBJECTIVE: Using quantifying adverbs. Many students find *too*, *very*, and *enough* extremely difficult. Read and discuss the introductory paragraphs and be sure the students understand what each of the three words means. Assign the page for independent written work; when students have finished, review and discuss the answers in class.

The Bill of Rights: Basic Freedoms

Read the article.

As you know, the Constitution of the United States is the plan for the American Government. When it was written, in 1787, it was sent to the states for approval. Two-thirds of the states had to approve it.

Many people liked the Constitution and wanted to have it approved immediately. Others, however, said that they would not approve it unless a list of the rights held by the people was attached to it. Such a "bill of rights" was part of most of the state constitutions, and these people believed strongly that the national Constitution should also have one.

Americans wanted their rights listed because, before the Revolution, the English government had taken away rights that the people believed they had. They did not want their new national government to do the same thing. They wanted to limit its power.

Because of this, the very first session of Congress, in 1789, proposed a series of amendments (changes) that listed rights that the people had. Ten of these amendments were ratified (approved) by the states and are known as the Bill of Rights.

Here are the rights that the first ten amendments give all Americans. Keep in mind that these rights apply to the national government, not to the state governments. Many of them, however, have been *extended* or *applied* to the states as well as to the national government.

1. The first amendment says that there will be no official, national religion, and that people can practice whatever religion they choose. It also says that people can say what they want to say and print what they want to print. It says that they can meet together peacefully and protest anything they think is unfair.
2. The second amendment says that the national government cannot stop people from keeping arms (guns, etc.). (This amendment was written to make sure that "militias" or citizen armies would be ready to defend the people.)
3. The third amendment prohibits the government from forcing citizens to have to let soldiers live in their homes. (The English had made people do this in the years before the Revolution.)
4. The fourth amendment says that police officers must have a warrant—an order from a judge—before they can search a person's house or property or before they can take away any thing or any person. The warrant must tell exactly what place is to be searched, and what or who is to be taken.
5. The fifth amendment guarantees that a person will get a fair trial. It says that nobody can be forced to give evidence against himself or herself, and that nobody can be imprisoned or put to death unless that person has been tried and convicted by a court that follows the laws of the United States. It also says that if the government has to take away a person's land or house, it must pay the person a fair price.
6. The sixth amendment says that a person who has been accused of a crime has a right to a speedy trial, in public, by a jury. It says that the person will be told exactly what he or she is accused of and will know who is testifying against him or her. It also says that the person is entitled to call witnesses and to have a lawyer.
7. The seventh amendment guarantees that a person can have a trial by jury in cases where there is no crime but where one person is suing another.
8. The eighth amendment says that cruel or unusual punishments will not be given to a person. It says that he or she cannot be forced to pay unreasonably high fines or bail. (Bail is money that is paid to temporarily allow a person's release from jail and to guarantee that the person will be in court for his or her trial. If the person does not come to court, the bail becomes the property of the government. If he or she does come to court, the bail is returned.)
9. The ninth amendment says that the people have many other rights besides those listed. It says that just because a right isn't listed doesn't mean that it is less important than those that are listed.
10. The tenth amendment says that any powers that are not given to the national government by the Constitution or that are not prohibited to the states by the Constitution belong to the states or to the people. This means that the national government cannot suddenly take powers that are not listed or implied in the Constitution.

(Go on to the next page.)

SKILL OBJECTIVES: Reading for main ideas and details; building vocabulary. Before reading the article, ask students what they know about the Bill of Rights. Do they know of other countries that provide a similar guarantee of freedoms? Preview the following vocabulary: *approval, proposed, amendments, ratified, protest, forbid, guarantee, accused, testify, suing, jury, prohibit.* Then assign the page for independent reading and provide help as needed.

Now answer the questions and do the exercises below.

1. Why did many people demand that a bill of rights should be added to the Constitution? Circle your answer.

    a. They were afraid that the English would take away their rights.
    b. They knew that the state constitutions had bills of rights.
    c. They wanted to limit the power of the national government.
    d. They wanted to strengthen what the national government could do.

2. Which amendment says that you do not have to answer a question in court if you think the answer could be used as evidence against you? _____

3. If a police officer asks to search your house, what must he or she have? Circle your answer.

    a. bail   b. a fair price   c. a plan   d. a warrant

4. Which amendment guarantees freedom of the press? _____

5. Which amendment says that you can call a meeting to protest something that the government is doing? _____

6. In 1789, when the Bill of Rights was written, the third amendment was considered to be very important. However, it has never been used. Why was it thought to be important then? Why did it turn out not to be important?

    _____
    _____
    _____
    _____
    _____
    _____

7. The first eight amendments all forbid the national government to do things, or guarantee that it will do certain things that it might not otherwise do. Why do you think the people wanted to put such limits on the government?

    _____
    _____
    _____
    _____
    _____
    _____

8. Now that you have read about the rights of citizens, think about the responsibilities of citizens. In your notebook, list some important responsibilities that citizens in a democracy have.

SKILL OBJECTIVES: Locating specific information; drawing conclusions; making inferences; writing paragraphs. After the students read the article on page 96, assign this page for independent written work. Allow class time for oral discussions of students' answers. Provide a copy of the Bill of Rights in its original language for students to refer to. *Extension Activity:* Have students research the campaign to get the Constitution ratified.

In the Newspaper: Real Estate

Language Objectives
Answer questions about a real-estate article and real-estate advertisements. Interpret and write real-estate advertisements.

In some newspapers, Real Estate is listed in the index as a separate section. In other papers, the Real Estate section is included in the Classified section. The Real Estate section contains advertisements for houses and apartments that are for sale or rent. A special language is used in real estate ads—the language of abbreviations. The box below lists some of the most common real estate abbreviations. Use the dictionary to look up any unfamiliar words.

apt.	apartment	elev.	elevator	kit.	kitchen	renov.	renovated
avail.	available	fl.	floor	lge.	large	rm.	room
bdrm.	bedroom	furn.	furnished	mod.	modern	std.	studio
bldg.	building	gar.	garage	mo.	month	stv.	stove
dinrm.	dining room	htd.	heated	nec.	necessary	util.	utilities
dep.	deposit	hw.	hot water	pkg.	parking	ww.	wall-to-wall carpet
dw.	dishwasher	incl.	included	refrig.	refrigerator	yd.	yard

A Rewrite the real estate advertisements below in unabbreviated English.

Afton—Lge. mod. apt. 2-bdrm. ww. dw. gar. $1,280 mo. 763-0496.

_____

Newton—Std. 3rd fl. elev. mod. bldg. htd. $995 mo. 944-3201 after 5 pm.

_____

Cranford—6 rm. renov. dinrm. lge. kit. Ht/hw. incl. $1,685 mo. 962-4400.

_____

Everett—3 rm. apt. all util. Private pkg. Avail. 6/1 Dep. nec. $800 mo. 339-3876.

_____

B Rewrite these advertisements in abbreviated form.

Arlington—Furnished apartment, two bedrooms, large kitchen, nice yard. No utilities. $1,150 a month. 442-1197.

_____

Concord—One-room apartment, wall-to-wall carpeting. Heated, modern building. Available May 1. $850 a month. 942-7601.

_____

Berlin—Modern two-bedroom apartment, fourth floor in renovated building. New stove and refrigerator. Heat and hot water included. $1,200 a month. 665-4311.

_____

C In your notebook, write an advertisement for an apartment you would like to rent. Use real estate abbreviations.

(Go on to the next page.)

SKILL OBJECTIVES: Interpreting real estate advertising; understanding and using abbreviations. Read the introductory paragraph. Allow sufficient time for students to familiarize themselves with the abbreviations in the box. Go over the directions for each of the three parts, and be sure students understand what they are to do, then assign the page for independent work. *Extension Activity:* Have students get real estate ads from local newspapers and compare the rents on this page with those in their own area.

The Real Estate section of a newspaper contains more than just ads for renting and buying. There are also articles about apartments and houses. Read the following article, then answer the questions.

LOOK BEFORE YOU LEAP

So, you're looking for your first apartment? This is a time for careful decisions. Don't be afraid of the realtor or landlord. Ask lots of questions. Find out as much as you can about your new home before you sign a lease and move in. Here are some important points to consider.

1. What is the noise level in the building? You may be living next door to a struggling trumpet player who practices until 3:00 a.m. Or you may love to play your saxophone late at night. Will there be problems? Are there young children in the building who cry all night? Ask questions. You may want to drive by the building late at night a couple of times during the week.

2. How is the electrical system? With old wiring you sometimes cannot run an air conditioner and a hair dryer at the same time without blowing a fuse. Make sure that the electrical system is right for your needs.

3. What about the windows? Do they open easily and close tightly? You'll be glad you checked out this little detail when the summer heat comes or a winter blizzard hits.

4. The kitchen can be a major problem area. Make sure that the sink drains properly and that the ceiling is in good shape. Dark patches or spots on the ceiling often indicate leaks from the kitchen above. While you're in the kitchen, check the refrigerator. Close the refrigerator door on a piece of paper. Let the paper stick out. If the paper falls out, then warm air is getting into the refrigerator. You will have higher electric bills and will need to defrost more often.

Go slowly when you are looking for a new apartment or house to rent. Check and recheck the facts. Make sure that it is the right place for you and that you are getting the most for your money.

1. What does the expression, "Look before you leap" mean? _____

_____

2. Tone is the mood or attitude a writer communicates in his or her writing. What is the tone of this article? Circle the answer.

   a. anxious, without much hope   **c.** suspicious and angry

   b. comical and witty   **d.** cautious advice

3. What is a realtor? (Use a dictionary if you need to.) _____

_____

4. What is a lease? _____

5. Why should you check the noise level of the apartment building? _____

_____

6. What is often a problem with a weak electrical system? _____

_____

7. What should you check for in the kitchen? _____

8. What additional advice would you give to new apartment renters? _____

_____

SKILL OBJECTIVES: Locating specific information; understanding figurative language; establishing tone. Read the introductory paragraph (or have it read) and emphasize that many newspapers carry articles about real estate as well as advertising. Have the article read, then discuss students' (and their families') experiences with houses or apartments. Reread the article aloud to help students establish tone. Then assign the questions for independent written work.

99

Picture It

Discuss the three men in the photograph with several classmates. Share your answers to the questions. Then write a paragraph about the picture in your notebook. Include your ideas about the five questions.

1. When do you think this photo was taken?

2. Who are these people?

3. Where are they?

4. What happened?

5. What is going to happen next?

SKILL OBJECTIVES: Discussing and interpreting a photograph; writing a descriptive paragraph. Allow ample discussion of the people in the photograph. Encourage differences of opinion. Write important vocabulary on the board as it comes out in the discussion. Then have students write their paragraphs.

100

Dear Dot

Dear Dot,
 Recently a boy named Mario sent his friend Rick to ask my girlfriend Suzy if I liked him (Mario). Suzy asked me and I said, "Yes." She told Rick and Rick told Mario. Now Mario has asked me out on a date—sort of. He did the same thing as before. He asked his friend to ask my friend if I would go out with him. I said I wouldn't unless he asked me himself. He hasn't asked, and I would really like to go out on a date with him. Should I ask Suzy to ask Rick what happened?
 Wondering

Discuss each of the questions in class. Then write your answers.

1. What is the correct way to ask someone out on a date? _____
   _____

2. What does "mature" mean? _____

3. Do you think these students are being mature? Why or why not? _____
   _____

4. Do you think Wondering was right to insist that Mario ask her out himself? Why or why not?
   _____
   _____

5. What do you think happened? _____
   _____

6. What should Wondering do now? _____
   _____

Write About It

Now put yourself in Dot's place. Write a helpful answer to Wondering. Remember, you want to help solve the problem, not make fun of the writer or criticize her.

Dear Wondering,
   _____
   _____
   _____
   _____
   _____
   _____

SKILL OBJECTIVES: Reading for main idea; making judgments; predicting outcomes; expressing opinions in writing. Have students read the letter; be sure they understand the sequence described; you may want to have someone diagram it on the board. Discuss each question in class; point out that item 2 is a review of a term used in an earlier letter (page 39). Encourage dialogue; be sure students support their opinions. Then have them write their answers and a letter to "Wondering."

Sometimes we do things that don't seem completely reasonable. We use the phrase *even though* to show that we know there are reasons why we shouldn't do what we have chosen to do. Look at the example below.

Even though it was past midnight, I decided to call my parents.

A Write the letter of the phrase from the list on the right that best completes each sentence. Use each letter once only. The first one is done for you.

1. Even though I'm on a diet, _____c_____

2. Even though I knew I had a test this morning, _____

3. Even though I can't afford it, _____

4. Even though I'm afraid of heights, _____

5. Even though I might get fired, _____

6. Even though I don't have a date, _____

7. Even though I broke my leg, _____

8. Even though I'm tired, _____

9. Even though I felt well, _____

10. Even though I've already seen that movie twice, _____

a. I'm going to stay up a little longer.

b. I'm going to the prom.

c. I'm going to have some fudge.

d. I'm going to buy that expensive sweater.

e. I went to the doctor for a check up.

f. I'm going to Lori's birthday party.

g. I didn't study last night.

h. I'd like to see it again.

i. I took a chairlift to the top of the mountain.

j. I'm going to complain to the boss about this.

B You can reverse the order of the phrases in a sentence using *even though*, without changing the meaning of the sentence. Look at the example.

Even though I knew it was wrong, I read my sister's diary.

I read my sister's diary, even though I knew it was wrong.

Complete the following sentences with an *even though* phrase. The *even though* phrase should give an argument against doing the thing you have chosen to do. The first one is done for you.

1. I'm going to make supper, _even though I'm not hungry._

2. I did my homework, _____.

3. I'm taking a trip to Hawaii, _____.

4. I'm going to wear my new suit, _____.

5. I'm going to have a good time, _____.

6. I took the money, _____.

7. I wanted to watch the late night movie on TV, _____.

8. I voted for Tony Randolph, _____.

SKILL OBJECTIVES: Forming *even though* clauses; predicting outcomes. Read and discuss the introductory paragraph. When students show they understand the contradictory nature of *even though* sentences, assign Part A as independent work; later, have students read the complete (matched) sentences aloud. *Part B:* Allow time for students to share their different answers. You may wish to have students write more than one completer clause for each statement.

What Should He Have Done?

Language Objective
Solve problems by telling what people should have done.

A

Tom went to Miami two weeks ago. He flew from Chicago and stayed for five days. He had a terrible time. Why did Tom have a terrible time?

1. He forgot to make a hotel reservation before he left. He had a hard time finding a room in a good hotel.

2. He packed only summer clothes because he thought Miami would be very warm. The temperature in Miami never went above 50°F that week.

3. His money was stolen from his hotel room. He didn't have any credit cards.

4. He didn't lock the door of the car he had rented. Someone stole the car.

5. At the end of his vacation, he arrived at the airport too late. The plane for Chicago had already left.

What should Tom have done? Look at the list above and write five sentences. The first one is done for you.

1. _He should have made a hotel reservation before he left._

2. _____

3. _____

4. _____

5. _____

B

Mike is a terrible mechanic because he can't follow directions. Yesterday, Jane took her car to Mike's Repair Shop. She gave Mike the list of directions below, but Mike didn't read the list carefully. Mike worked on the car for two hours, but he didn't do anything Jane asked. What did Mike do instead?

<u>Jane's List</u>
1. Change the oil.
2. Fix the brakes.
3. Repair the window.
4. Install a muffler.

1. He changed the tires.
2. He fixed the clutch.
3. He repaired the door.
4. He installed a battery.

What should Mike have done? What shouldn't he have done? Write four pairs of sentences. The first one is done for you. Use it as a model.

1. _He should have changed the oil._

    He shouldn't have changed the tires.

2. _____

    _____

3. _____

    _____

4. _____

    _____

SKILL OBJECTIVES: Using past modals; problem solving. *Part A:* Read the anecdotal paragraphs aloud, and call attention to the sample answer; elicit that it goes with item 1 above, and review the structural change. Assign items 2 through 5. *Part B:* Follow the same procedure. Point out that each item requires two sentences, one positive and one negative. Review all answers for both parts orally when students have completed the page.

103

I Wonder Why

The four phrases below are often used to make statements and draw conclusions about past situations. Look at the chart.

Language Objective
State conclusions, possibilities, and obligations using modals.

	Example	**Meaning**
might have + past participle	He might have seen it.	it's possible
must have + past participle	She must have gone home.	it seems certain
could have + past participle	They could have tried harder. He could have gotten lost.	1. was (were) able to 2. it's possible
should have + past participle	You should have called first.	it was the right thing to do.

A **Write a sentence responding to the following statements. Begin each sentence with one of the phrases from above. The first one is done for you.**

1. Jim caught a cold last week, but he went skiing anyway. Now he's sick.

   He should have stayed home.

2. I wonder why Charles climbed in the window to his house last night.

   _____

3. Mr. Stravinsky forgot to pay the oil bill last month. The oil company stopped delivering oil to his house.

   _____

4. I wonder why Jennifer didn't come to class all last week.

   _____

5. When I got up this morning and looked out the window, the streets looked wet.

   _____

6. My mother's birthday was yesterday. I forgot to buy her a present. She was disappointed.

   _____

Look at the three sentences below. Each has a slightly different meaning.

I could have gotten up earlier.   (I was able to.)

I would have gotten up earlier.   (I certainly would have.)

I might have gotten up earlier.   (Maybe I would have.)

B **Finish these sentences. Use *could have, would have*, or *might have*.**

1. I'm sorry I didn't send you a post card from Miami. If I had known your address, _____

   _____

2. The weather was terrible on our vacation and no one went near the water. If the weather had been better, _____

3. Marco didn't study for the test. He flunked it. If he had studied for the test, _____

   _____

SKILL OBJECTIVES: Using past modals; drawing conclusions. Review the meanings of the modals in the chart. *Part A:* Do the first three sentences orally, soliciting different answers for items 2 and 3. Then assign as independent written work. *Part B:* Be sure students understand the differences in meaning among *could, would,* and *might.* Do the three sentences orally, and encourage different answers. Then assign as independent written work.

If We Had Known . . .

Language Objective
Predict what people will do under particular conditions.

Read the two sentences below.

> If Susan had known about the party, she would have gone to it.
> If Tom had studied more, he might have passed the test.

These two sentences are in the past conditional. The past conditional is used to discuss things that could have happened, but didn't. The "If . . ." phrase uses the past perfect (*had known, had studied*); the other phrase uses *would have, could have,* or *might have* + a past participle. Now answer these questions.

1. Did Susan go to the party? _____

   Why or why not? _____

2. Did Tom pass the test? _____

   Why or why not? _____

A | **Read the story, then complete the sentences below. The first one is done for you.**

Bob had planned to go to Europe. He wanted to visit France, Italy, Spain, and England. *But* the day before he was going to leave, he broke his leg and couldn't take his vacation. Poor Bob! Think of all he missed.

1. If Bob had gone to France, _he could have seen the Eiffel Tower._

2. If he had gone to Italy, _____

3. If he had gone to Spain, _____

4. If he had gone to England, _____

5. If he hadn't broken his leg, _____

B | **Write a past conditional sentence responding to each of the following situations. The first one is done for you. Use it as a model.**

1. Ramon didn't hear his alarm clock ring this morning. He got up late.

   If Ramon had heard the alarm clock, he would have been on time.

2. I didn't have your address with me while I was on vacation. I couldn't send you a postcard.

   _____

3. I forgot to take my umbrella this morning. I got wet.

   _____

4. Tim and Roberto had a terrible time on their vacation. The weather was rainy and cold and they couldn't go swimming, sailing, or water skiing.

   _____

SKILL OBJECTIVES: Using past modals; understanding cause and effect; predicting outcomes. Discuss the time sequence of the first past perfect/conditional sentences. Ask what should have happened first; compare it with what actually did happen (in the students' opinions) in each sentence. Then have students look at the illustration, read the anecdotal paragraph, and complete Part A. *Part B:* Be sure students understand the instructions and the "done for you" sentence, then assign as independent written work.

What If?

A You have learned about three different kinds of *if* clauses. Use what you have learned to answer the following questions. Use the examples of each kind as a guide for writing your answers. Your answers may differ from other students'. That's all right. Just be sure they follow the pattern and make sense.

Example: What will you do if your brother loses his glasses?

If my brother loses his glasses, I'll help him find them.

1. What will you do if the store is closed?

2. What will you do if you hurt yourself?

3. What will you do if it's hot tomorrow?

4. What will you do if the phone rings?

5. What will you do if you don't understand?

6. What will you do if it rains?

Example: What would you do if you forgot your notebook?

If I forgot my notebook, I would call my friend for the information.

7. What would you do if someone punched you in the nose?

8. What would you do if your watch broke?

9. What would you do if you were thirsty?

10. What would you do if you were deaf?

11. What would you do if you lost all your money?

12. What would you do if you were a millionaire?

(Go on to the next page.)

SKILL OBJECTIVES: Sequencing tenses with *if*; proposing possible solutions to problems. *Part A:* Review the sequence of tenses with *if*; call attention to the examples before items 1 and 7. Assign the page for independent written work, then review answers orally.

Example: What would you have done if you had won the car?

If I had won the car, I would have screamed my head off!

13. What would you have done if you had seen the accident?

_____

14. What would you have done if you had burned your hand?

_____

15. What would you have done if you had left your keys in the car?

_____

16. What country would you have visited if you had planned the trip yourself?

_____

17. What would you have done if a mad dog had bitten you?

_____

18. What would you have done if you had missed the bus?

_____

B **Choose the correct form of the verb in parentheses and write it in the blank. The first one is done for you.**

1. If John (have) _____ _has_ _____ enough money, he'll come with us.

2. If today (be) _____ Saturday, I would be home now.

3. If the weather (be) _____ nice yesterday, we would have gone swimming.

4. If I (have) _____ a million dollars, I'd take a trip around the world.

5. If Rodrigo had gone to Paris last summer, he (see) _____ the Eiffel Tower.

6. If Americans (exercise) _____ more, they'd be in better physical condition.

7. If Pierre (get) _____ up earlier, he wouldn't have missed the bus.

8. If Consuelo (go) _____ to Washington, D.C. she might see the President.

9. If you park next to a bus stop you, (get) _____ a ticket.

10. If I were stuck in an elevator, I (call) _____ for help.

In the Newspaper: the Movies

A The movies being shown in your area are usually listed in the newspaper. A schedule tells what films are playing at each theater, and what times the movies begin. Sometimes information is given about ticket prices or reduced prices for special days and early shows. Read the movie schedule, then answer the questions.

Barton Creek Cinema 10
A Home at the End of the World (R) 7:20 pm, 10:00 pm
The Day After Tomorrow (PG-13) 4:00 pm, 6:45 pm
Spy Kids 3-D: Game Over (PG) 10:00 am, 2:00 pm
A Cinderella Story (PG) 11:10 am, 1:45 pm, 4:15 pm

Regal Westgate 11
Catwoman (PG-13) 11:50 am, 2:30 pm, 5:05 pm, 7:50 pm, 10:20 pm
Collateral (R) 3:00 pm, 6:45 pm, 7:25 pm, 8:00 pm, 9:45 pm
Manchurian Candidate (R) 12:05 pm, 3:10 pm, 6:30 pm, 9:35 pm
Spider-Man 2 (PG-13) 12:00 pm, 1:40 pm, 3:15 pm, 6:30 pm

AMC Barton Creek Square 14
I'll Sleep When I'm Dead (R) 5:10 pm, 7:40 pm, 9:55 pm
I, Robot (PG-13) 1:30 pm, 4:20 pm, 7:15 pm, 9:50 pm
Last Flight Out (PG) 1:00 pm, 3:05 pm, 5:15 pm, 7:20 pm, 9:25 pm

Alamo Drafthouse Cinema
Shrek 2 (PG) 1:10 pm, 3:25 pm, 5:45 pm
Thunderbirds Are GO (PG) 1:05 pm, 3:20 pm, 5:40 pm
The Village (PG-13) 1:00 pm, 2:30 pm, 3:30 pm, 4:15 pm, 5:00 pm
Al Otro Lado (PG) 7:10 pm, 9:50 pm

Dobie Theaters
The Bourne Supremacy (PG-13) 2:35 pm, 7:50 pm, 10:25 pm
Spider-Man 2 (PG-13) 1:00 pm, 7:00 pm, 10:10 pm

1. Which film is probably in Spanish with English subtitles? _____

2. Which films could you see in the evening after dinner? _____

_____

3. Which films could you see in the morning? _____

_____

4. Which films require an adult accompanying a child (PG-13)? _____

_____

5. Which films are the sequels? _____

B How do you decide which movies to see? The Entertainment section often includes reviews written by movie critics. A critic describes the movie briefly, then gives his or her opinion about it. Of course, you will not always agree with the critic, but reading movie reviews often helps people choose films they will enjoy. Read the review, then answer the questions.

Can't Pay the Rent is the fourth film from director Zachary Christopher. With any luck at all, it will be his last. This alleged comedy is the story of a mild-mannered urban couple, Paul and Joanna Parkins, who rent the upstairs apartment of their home to a four-man rock band.

The few laughs that this film generates come from watching Joanna and Paul cope with the constant loud practice of the band. They wear earmuffs while dining by candlelight, and pantomime messages to one another over the rock-music roar. While some of this is funny, Paul's pantomime of the phone message, "Your brother has been hit by a car," is tasteless. It definitely isn't funny.

As for the "musicians," they are truly terrible. In the film, they are called "Make a Wish," and if mine had come true, the sound system would have broken down at the beginning of their first song.

To get the band out of the house, Paul becomes their manager. The ensuing nonsense and the unconvincing happy ending make this film totally unappealing. *Can't Pay the Rent* can't cut the mustard.

(Go on to the next page.)

1. Did the critic like the film? _____ What sentence first tells you the critic's opinion?
   _____

2. What does the critic mean by calling this film an "alleged" comedy?
   _____

3. How do you "pantomime" a message?
   _____

4. What do you think happens at the end of this film?
   _____

5. What does the final sentence of this review mean? Restate it in your own words.
   _____

6. What is the tone (the writer's attitude or feelings) in this review? Circle the answer.
   a. constructive and understanding   **c.** disappointed and very critical
   b. confused and unhappy   **d.** clever, witty, and humorous

C **Here is a review of the same film by a different critic.**

Walk, run, jog, or drive, but hurry to the theater and see *Can't Pay the Rent*. This is the fourth and funniest of Zachary Christopher's films. He is clearly the latest Hollywood genius, and this film is going to ensure his reputation; it's going to be a blockbuster. It's the funniest movie that I have seen in years.

The story begins when Paul and Joanna Parkins rent their upstairs apartment to a rock group. The quiet couple get more than they bargained for with this noisy but excellent gang of musicians. Rather than hurt the band's feelings, however, the couple decide to cope with the noise and rowdiness that have taken over their peaceful home.

The scenes that show Paul and Joanna eating elegant dinners with earmuffs, or pantomiming telephone messages over the noise of the band, are howlingly funny. I haven't seen this kind of comic acting in years, and I wouldn't be surprised to see both Suzanne Winters as Joanna, and John Zimblast as Paul, receive Oscar nominations.

The hit musical group, Diamond, plays the band in the film. They are excellent, as always, and they sing their hit song, "Moonlighting," in the film. Between the laughs, the good music, and the happy ending, this is a perfect night's entertainment; you couldn't ask for more. I recommend this film highly. Go see it—tonight!

1. Did this critic like the film? _____

2. Discuss three things the two critics disagree about in their reviews. _____
   _____
   _____

3. Describe the one scene both critics agree was funny. _____
   _____

4. What is the tone of this second review? Circle the answer.

   a. enthusiastic   **b.** surprised   **c.** disappointed   **d.** comic

5. Do you think you would enjoy seeing *Can't Pay the Rent*? Why or why not? _____
   _____
   _____

SKILL OBJECTIVES: Comparing and contrasting; establishing tone; reading for specific information. *Part C:* Have students read the second review and answer the questions about it. Then discuss the two reviews and their very different tones and opinions; reemphasize the difference between an opinion and a fact. *Extension Activity:* Have students find reviews of movies they have seen (or bring in reviews of currently popular movies) and discuss the opinions of the class as compared to those of the critics.

Which Movie?

You can often tell something about a movie from its title. Look at the movie schedule, then read the comments below. All of these people were dissatisfied with the movies they saw. Tell each person what movie he or she should have seen. Use complete sentences. The first one is done for you.

CINEMA ONE	CINEMA TWO	CINEMA THREE
Love in Rome	Invasion of the Extra-Terrestrials	Bonjour, Mon Ami
CINEMA FOUR	**CINEMA FIVE**	**CINEMA SIX**
Gunfight at Noon	Laugh a Minute	Speedway 400
CINEMA SEVEN	**CINEMA EIGHT**	**CINEMA NINE**
Happy Times, Happy Tunes	He Came to Help—The Roberto Clemente Story	The World at War

1. "I enjoyed *Speedway 400*, but I wish I had seen a comedy, something light and entertaining."

   You should have seen "Laugh a Minute."

2. "We didn't enjoy *Love in Rome*. We would have preferred a real foreign film, something very European, with subtitles."

   _____

3. *"Invasion of the Extra-Terrestrials* was fine, but I wish I had seen something more serious and historical, something with some real information."

   _____

4. *"Gunfight at Noon* was silly. I wish I had seen a biographical picture."

   _____

5. "I liked *Happy Times, Happy Tunes* but my sons were bored. They like cowboy and adventure films."

   _____

6. "I didn't understand *Bonjour, Mon Ami*. I guess I should stick with my favorite kind of movie—American musicals."

   _____

7. *"The Roberto Clemente Story* was wonderful, but sad. I wish I had seen a light romance, a love story with a happy ending."

   _____

8. *"The World at War* was much too serious for me. I wish I had seen a car-race movie—something with a lot of action but no big problems."

   _____

9. "I didn't think *Laugh a Minute* was funny. I wish I had seen a science-fiction movie full of hostile and scary space monsters."

   _____

SKILL OBJECTIVES: Classifying; using past modals; making inferences; suggesting alternative solutions. Discuss categories of movies with the class. Be sure they know terms such as *musical, western, biography, foreign film*, etc. Discuss the nine movies listed and help the group decide which classification each one belongs to, making inferences from the titles. Discuss the answer to item 1, then assign the rest of the page for independent written work.

Find the Error (2)

Language Objective
Detect and correct grammatical errors in sentences.

There is a grammatical error in one of the underlined words or phrases in each sentence below. Find the error and circle it. Then correct the error in the blank under the sentence. **The first one is done for you.**

1. When <u>the men</u> finished (to paint) the house, <u>they</u> cleaned <u>their brushes</u> and went home.
   <u>   painting   </u>

2. <u>Everyone</u> agreed that if Tom <u>would study</u> for the <u>chemistry</u> test, he would have passed it <u>easily</u>.
   _____

3. Carla and Pablo <u>don't</u> speak <u>Hindi</u> <u>at all</u>, and Ali doesn't <u>neither</u>.
   _____

4. Our university has the <u>most tallest</u> player <u>in</u> the league; he's <u>over</u> seven <u>feet</u> tall.
   _____

5. Even though I <u>have seen</u> that movie <u>already</u>, <u>but</u> I'd really like to see <u>it</u> again.
   _____

6. This book <u>is one of</u> the most <u>excited</u> that I <u>have read</u> in <u>a long time</u>.
   _____

7. <u>One thing I admire</u> about Susan is <u>that</u> she would rather <u>reading</u> a book <u>than</u> watch television.
   _____

8. Maria isn't sure <u>yet</u>, but <u>she's</u> thinking <u>to</u> going to the University of Chicago <u>next year</u>.
   _____

9. I'm <u>furious with</u> my mechanic; <u>he repaired the brakes</u> when he <u>should of</u> repaired <u>the</u> clutch.
   _____

10. <u>When Americans go to Canada</u>, they <u>had better to carry</u> a passport <u>or</u> some other official <u>means of identification</u>.
    _____

11. <u>Our</u> neighbor, Mr. Briggs, <u>used to heavy</u>, but <u>he went on a diet</u> and lost a lot of <u>weight</u>.
    _____

12. If I won a million dollars, I <u>will</u> take a <u>luxurious</u> trip <u>around the world</u> with my <u>best</u> friend.
    _____

13. I <u>felt sorry</u> for my little brother <u>last night</u>; he was <u>so</u> tired to finish <u>his</u> homework.
    _____

14. <u>Almudena's tutor</u> said that she <u>will</u> meet her <u>downstairs</u> in the cafeteria <u>at</u> 3:30.
    _____

15. <u>I've done</u> a lot of research, and <u>it seems that</u> a Cadillac is almost as expensive <u>than</u> a Lincoln Continental.
    _____

SKILL OBJECTIVES: Finding and correcting grammatical errors; preparing for standardized tests. Review the format of this page (it is identical with that of page 70). Remind students that this is similar to items on some standardized tests that they may take in the future. Work through item 1 with the class and have them tell why "to paint" was circled and "painting" was written. Remind them that they must provide both kinds of answers in each item: circle the error and write the correction. Assign the page for independent written work. Review all answers with the class, making sure students can find all answers and correct them.

Dear Dot

Language Objectives
Answer questions about a reading. Give advice. Agree or disagree with advice.

Dear Dot,

My parents flipped when they found out I went to an R-rated movie. (I am only fifteen.) They even threatened to go down to the movie theater and complain. Luckily, I talked them out of that. I would die if they made such a big fuss in public. Now they say that I have to tell them ahead of time what movie I'm going to see and I have to bring back the ticket stub to prove that I was at the correct theater. I think that they are making a mountain out of a molehill. The movie wasn't that different from what you see all the time on TV these days. How can I get Mom and Dad off my back?

Prisoner

Discuss each of the questions in class. Then write your answers.

1. What does "flipped" mean? _____

2. What does it mean if a film is rated "R"? _____
   _____

3. What kind of person is Prisoner? The tone and language of the letter may give you some clues. _____

4. Do you think Prisoner's parents' new rules are fair? Why or why not? _____
   _____

5. What does the expression "making a mountain out of a molehill" mean? _____
   _____

6. Do you think that parents have the right to censor movies for their teenage children (decide which films their children are not allowed to see)? Why or why not? _____
   _____

Write About It

Now put yourself in Dot's place. Write a helpful answer to Prisoner. Remember, you want to help solve the problem, not make fun of the writer or criticize.

   Dear Prisoner, _____
   _____
   _____
   _____
   _____
   _____

SKILL OBJECTIVES: Reading for main idea and details; understanding figurative language; making judgments; expressing opinions in writing. Have students read the letter. Discuss each question in class. Encourage as much discussion as possible, but be sure opinions are supported. Then have students write answers to the questions. Suggest they use these answers as the basis for their letters. You may wish to assign the letter-writing activity as homework.

Vocabulary Review

Circle the word that does <u>not</u> belong.

1. tennis   soccer   skating   ping-pong
2. older   oldest   quieter   bigger
3. gentle   kind   nice   historic
4. heavy   curious   interested   nosy
5. similar   particular   alike   same
6. comics   editorials   chapters   classifieds
7. shy   bashful   complicated   quiet
8. bad   better   worst   worse
9. carefully   quickly   slowly   friendly
10. electrician   mechanic   economics   accountant
11. mountain   earthquake   tornado   hurricane
12. taken   wrote   flown   seen
13. New York   New Jersey   New England   New Mexico
14. past   present   progress   future
15. killed   murdered   assassinated   conquered
16. license   rules   regulations   laws
17. cattle   corn   potatoes   wheat
18. kitten   puppy   tiger   colt
19. yen   pound   ounce   rupee
20. immature   studious   childish   juvenile
21. one   four   five   seven
22. frightening   amusing   terrifying   horrifying
23. careful   confident   secure   self-assured
24. own   owe   possess   hold
25. fix   repair   adjust   retain
26. criticize   praise   admire   adore
27. central   main   important   middle
28. incredible   cautious   astonishing   amazing
29. verb   noun   question   adjective
30. march   rich   which   stomach

Appendix: Parts of Speech

1. **Verbs** are usually action or thinking words. The verb is a main word in every sentence.
   Examples: *drink, believe, live, go, know, call, run*
   Auxiliary (helping) verbs help make a statement.
   Examples: *am, is, do, don't, can, may, should, will*

2. **Nouns** name a person, place, or thing. Examples: *daughter, country, tree*
   Proper nouns name a particular person, place, or thing. Examples: *Tom, Ohio, English*

3. **Adjectives** describe nouns. They tell what kind, how much, or how many.
   Examples: *lovely, blue, seven, several*
   Demonstrative adjectives point out which one. Examples: *this* book, *those* people
   Possessive adjectives tell who it belongs to.   Examples: *her, our, my, their*

4. **Adverbs** describe verbs. They tell how, where, when, and how often.
   Examples: *quickly, happily, very, today, there, sometimes, never, daily*

5. **Prepositions** are small words that give directions.
   Examples: *to, for, with, by, above, down, before, of*

6. **Pronouns** take the place of nouns. Examples: *I, you, he, she, it, him, us, them*
   Indefinite pronouns: Examples: *nobody, everyone, all, none*
   Demonstrative pronouns: Examples: *this, that, these, those*
   Possessive pronouns: Examples: *mine, hers, theirs*
   Reflexive pronouns: Examples: *himself, ourselves*
   Relative pronouns: Examples: *who, that, which*

7. **Articles** There are only three articles in English: *a, an, the*

8. **Conjunctions** join two words or parts of a sentence together.
   Examples: *and, but, if, so, or, although*

What part of speech is the underlined word in each sentence?

1. The cat <u>chased</u> the mouse.   _____

2. My friends are coming <u>tomorrow</u>.   _____

3. Your shoes are <u>under</u> the bed.   _____

4. The <u>worst</u> day of my life was when I moved here.   _____

5. <u>My</u> sister won the grand prize.   _____

6. The girl cut <u>herself</u> on the broken glass.   _____

7. We <u>could</u> visit your aunt.   _____

8. That's a good <u>question</u>.   _____

9. I heard <u>someone</u> come in.   _____

10. <u>These</u> children are from Greece.   _____

11. That's not <u>ours</u>.   _____

12. I walked home <u>because</u> my bike had been stolen.   _____

13. I left <u>it</u> at my house.   _____

14. <u>Alaska</u> is the largest state.   _____

15. A mechanic is someone <u>who</u> fixes cars.   _____

16. <u>That</u> isn't fair!   _____

17. The doctors performed <u>the</u> operation.   _____

18. The Declaration of Independence was written <u>in</u> 1776.   _____

APPENDIX: Parts of speech. Allow students time to review the parts of speech listed at the top of the page. Many students are unfamiliar with parts of speech even in their own language. Be prepared to complete the whole page as an oral exercise so that confused students can question and identify each underlined word. To challenge students more, have them copy the sentences on another piece of paper and label every word in each sentence with its correct part of speech.

End of Book Test: Completing Familiar Structures

Circle the best answer.

Example: Mary went to the library, but her friends _____ .

a. weren't   **(b. didn't)**   c. aren't   d. don't

1. French _____ in Haiti.

   a. speaks   b. is speaking   c. is spoken   d. spoke

2. John has been playing soccer _____ 10:00 this morning.

   a. until   b. since   c. for   d. to

3. My sister is _____ getting married next year.

   a. thinking to   b. thinking for   c. thinking of   d. thinking in

4. Susan was _____ to go to work yesterday.

   a. very sick   b. too much sick   c. sick enough   d. too sick

5. My car _____ from the parking lot last night.

   a. is stealing   b. was stolen   c. has stolen   d. was stealing

6. Can you tell me where _____ ?

   a. lives Mary   b. does Mary live   c. Mary does live   d. Mary lives

7. I _____ stay home than go to a movie.

   a. would rather   b. would like   c. could   d. should

8. I always enjoy _____ swimming.

   a. going   b. to go   c. to going   d. go

9. The Sears Tower is _____ building in Chicago.

   a. the most high   b. too high   c. the most highest   d. the highest

10. My father _____ me stories when I was a child.

    a. was used to read   b. used to read   c. use to read   d. used to reading

11. Martha will be very happy if she _____ all her exams.

    a. will pass   b. passed   c. passes   d. is passed

12. She's done her homework, _____ ?

    a. isn't she   b. hasn't she   c. didn't she   d. wasn't she

13. If the weather had been nicer, May and Fred _____ swimming.

    a. should have gone   b. could have gone   c. went   d. have gone

14. Joe felt terrible yesterday because he _____ too much the night before.

    a. had eaten   b. has eaten   c. was eaten   d. had been eating

15. If I _____ you needed a car, I would've lent you mine.

    a. will know that   b. know that   c. had known that   d. have known that

END OF BOOK TEST: Completing familiar structures. The following pages will help you evaluate each student's strengths and weaknesses. Review directions and examples with the class, then assign the pages as independent work. Remind students to try each answer choice in the blank space to determine which choice is correct. Students should circle their answers.

115

16. If I made $30,000 a year, I _____ pay $6,000 in income tax.

    a. would   **b.** had to   **c.** used to   **d.** will

17. It's difficult to understand the teacher because she speaks _____.

    a. faster   **b.** very quick   **c.** very quickly   **d.** fastly

18. I wish that I _____ speak English well.

    a. could   **b.** would   **c.** should   **d.** might

19. I've never seen the movie *To Kill a Mockingbird*, and _____.

    a. either Joe has   **b.** neither has Joe   **c.** Joe hasn't neither   **d.** Joe has either

20. If Alice went to bed earlier, she _____ look so tired.

    a. wouldn't   **b.** couldn't   **c.** shouldn't   **d.** didn't use to

21. How many people _____ to your party?

    a. have you been invited   **b.** you have invited   **c.** have you invited   **d.** have invited you

22. If you _____ to Washington, D.C., you might see the President.

    a. would go   **b.** go   **c.** will go   **d.** had gone

23. Since I've been in the United States, I _____ a lot of hamburgers.

    a. was eaten   **b.** should eat   **c.** have eaten   **d.** did eat

24. Robert had a bad headache last night and _____.

    a. so did I   **b.** I also had   **c.** so I had   **d.** neither did I

25. Janet and Lynn _____ go sailing because it was windy.

    a. weren't   **b.** may not   **c.** could not   **d.** would rather not

26. That car isn't _____ to drive.

    a. enough safe   **b.** safe neither   **c.** safe either   **d.** safe enough

27. Jim left class early because he _____ go to work.

    a. had to   **b.** would   **c.** would have gone   **d.** had

28. My grades have been bad lately; I think I _____ study more.

    a. would   **b.** had   **c.** should   **d.** have

29. I don't know when _____.

    a. begins next semester   **c.** does next semester begin

    b. does begin next semester   **d.** next semester begins

30. The teacher _____ to write a composition.

    a. told to us   **b.** told us   **c.** said us   **d.** said to us

END OF BOOK TEST: Completing familiar structures. See annotations on page 115.

116

End of Book Test: Completing Familiar Structures (Continued)

B **Read each sentence. Write the correct form of the verb on the line.**

Example: Last night we (see) _saw_ the President's speech on TV.

1. Alexander Graham Bell (invent) _____ the telephone in 1898.

2. My cousin (live) _____ in Rome since 1998.

3. Wendy usually (do) _____ her laundry on Fridays.

4. I (read) _____ the newspaper when, suddenly, the lights went out.

5. A substitute teacher (teach) _____ our class yesterday.

6. My parents (give) _____ me a car for my birthday next year.

7. I (be) _____ a student for fourteen years.

8. The Statue of Liberty (give) _____ to the United States by France.

9. They said that they (go) _____ to the exhibition twice already.

10. The Help Wanted ads (find) _____ in the Classified section.

Answer to the puzzle on page 25.

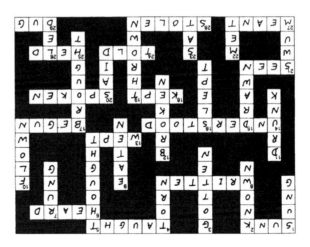

Answers to the riddle on page 69, Section D:

He <u>got cold feet</u>.

(**1.** long **2.** gold **3.** pieces **4.** fat **5.** take)

Answers to the problems on page 76:		**Answers to the problems on page 88:**		
1. 45	**5.** $714,000	**1. a.** $2.50	**b.** $52.50	**5.** $3,844
2. .200 .250 .305 .324	**6.** 70 miles	**2. a.** $12.30	**b.** $94.30	**6.** $30.00
3. $1,447.50	**7.** .89 seconds	**3. a.** $480	**b.** $3,520	**7.** $5,250
4. 1,125 yards	**8.** 74; 96; 107; 81	**4. a.** $1,240	**b.** $16,740	

END OF BOOK TEST: Completing familiar structures (continued). Read the directions with the students. Call attention to the example and elicit that the past tense of the verb is required because of the clue *last night*.

End of Book Test: Reading Comprehension

Read the article.

Spaceships travel around the earth, go to the moon, and return home safely. The astronauts carry important supplies with them on the spaceship—food, water, and air. Sometimes there are problems on the spaceship, and the astronauts have to understand how the spaceship works in order to repair it.

In a way, all of us are really on a spaceship, the planet Earth. We move around the sun at 18 miles per second and never stop. On our spaceship we have six billion people and a limited supply of air, water, and land. These supplies, just like the limited supplies on the astronauts' spaceship, have to be used carefully because we can't buy new air, water, or land from anywhere else. Everyone needs air, water, and land to live—this is our environment.

The environment on our planet is a closed system; nothing new is ever added. Nature recycles its resources. Water, for example, evaporates and rises as invisible droplets to form clouds. This same water returns to the Earth as rain or snow. The rain that falls today is actually the same water that fell on the dinosaurs 70 million years ago.

Today, the Earth is in trouble. Factories pour dirty water into our rivers. Many fish die and the water becomes unhealthy for people to drink. Cars and factories put poisons into the air and cause plants, animals, and people to get sick. People throw bottles and paper out of their car windows, and the roadside becomes covered with litter. Over the years, people have changed the environment. We have poured back into the land, air, and water more wastes than nature can clean. So we have pollution.

To continue to survive, we must learn how to use the Earth's resources wisely, without destroying them. We have to change our habits and stop dumping such enormous amounts of industrial waste into the water and air. To save the spaceship Earth, we must cooperate with nature and learn better ways to use, not abuse, our environment.

A **Circle the best answer.**

1. The best title for this article would be
   - **a.** Water Pollution
   - **b.** The Spaceship Earth
   - **c.** Traveling in Space
   - **d.** Problems of Astronauts

2. The population at present is approximately
   - **a.** six billion
   - **b.** seventy million
   - **c.** fourteen million
   - **d.** fourteen billion

3. Which of the following is *not* an example of a recycled resource?
   - **a.** air
   - **b.** water
   - **c.** cars
   - **d.** land

4. Water is recycled
   - **a.** every million years
   - **b.** from outside the atmosphere
   - **c.** continually
   - **d.** from other resources

5. The planet Earth travels around the sun at almost
   - **a.** 30 miles per second
   - **b.** 70 miles per second
   - **c.** 10 miles per second
   - **d.** 20 miles per second

6. The author feels that _____.
   - **a.** someday everyone will be an astronaut and live on a spaceship
   - **b.** the Earth will disappear when we have used up our resources
   - **c.** trips to other planets will cause more pollution
   - **d.** we must stop abusing the environment

   (Go on to the next page.)

END OF BOOK TEST: Reading comprehension. Allow students ample time to read and reread the article and to answer the questions. The entire page is to be completed independently by the students.

B Decide whether each of these statements is true or false. If it is true, circle *T*. If it is false, circle *F*.

1. Industrial waste is a type of pollution.   T   F

2. Dinosaurs lived seventy billion years ago.   T   F

3. Snow is an example of recycled water.   T   F

4. An empty bottle left in the woods is an example of litter.   T   F

5. Nature cleans all the wastes we pour back into it.   T   F

C Finish these sentences.

1. The author compares a spaceship to the planet Earth in this article because

   _____

   _____

2. To improve our environment we have to _____

   _____

3. We have pollution because _____

   _____

4. Two negative effects of water pollution are _____

   _____

5. The word *recycle* means _____

   _____

6. The word *litter* means _____

   _____

7. The word *cooperate* means _____

   _____

8. The word *abuse* means _____

   _____

END OF BOOK TEST: Reading comprehension (continued). See annotations on page 118.

119

Index of Language Objectives